THE BIRTH OF THE GODS
The Origin of Primitive Beliefs

THE BIRTH OF THE GODS

The Origin of Primitive Beliefs

by GUY E. SWANSON

ANN ARBOR

THE UNIVERSITY OF MICHIGAN PRESS

For L. G. Wayne Furman

PREFACE

These studies were undertaken because I wanted to discuss the social organization of religion and ethics with my students and could find little in the way of tested explanations for the most basic phenomena. It is true that one could fill a sizable library with the studies which describe religious beliefs and organizations, or which comment on them. By contrast, it would take but a single shelf to hold all the books which, from the view of natural science, contain distinctive explanations of religion's nature and origins.

On that shelf would be a monograph by Emile Durkheim entitled *The Elementary Forms of the Religious Life*. Like many other sociologists and social psychologists, I have found this book one of the most stimulating in all the literature about society. Its point of view is part of the foundation on which I have built.

The study of religion is a specialty to which many scholars have devoted all of their professional lives. The intensive study of a few primitive societies requires a similarly extended effort. It is, therefore, with a sharp sense of the inadequacy of my preparation, that I offer some findings concerning religion among the simpler peoples although I cannot claim specialized knowledge about religion or anthropology. I can but repeat Max Weber's sentiments when faced with a similar situation at the publication of his study *Ancient Judaism:*

It would require more than a lifetime to acquire a true mastery of the literature . . . especially since this literature is of exceptionally high quality. . . .

From the outset . . . we entertain but modest hopes of contributing anything essentially new to the discussion, apart from the fact that, here and there, some source data may be grouped in a manner to emphasize some things differently than usual. . . . —Max Weber, *Ancient Judaism*, H. H. Gerth and D. Martindale, tr. (Glencoe, Ill.: The Free Press, 1952), 425.

I recognize also that certain scholars will feel ambivalent about an investigation of religion which begins with some ideas about the nature of religious experience. So distinguished an anthropologist as Dr. Evans-Pritchard has written:

. . . generalizations about "religion" are discreditable. They are always too ambitious and take account of only a few of the facts. The anthropologist should be both more modest and more scholarly. He should restrict himself to religions of a certain type or of related peoples, or to particular problems of religious thought and practice. . . . Sweeping generalizations reached by dialectical analysis of concepts . . . [should be] abandoned in favour of limited conclusions reached by inductive analysis of observed facts. . . . —E. E. Evans-Pritchard, "Religion," in E. E. Evans-Pritchard and others (eds.), *The Institutions of Primitive Society* (Glencoe, Ill.: The Free Press, 1954), 6–7.

One can only agree with his warning that our explanations fall short of accounting for all the facts or even, in many cases, for most of them. At the same time, the existence of generalizations can provide fruitful direction for descriptive research, just as careful and detailed depictions of social life stimulate generalizations. The movement of scientific knowledge requires both, and both should have the resources to play their equally indispensable parts.

The Faculty Research Fund of The University of Michigan provided me with money for research assistance. The Center for Advanced Study in the Behavioral Sciences freed my time to analyze the data and write this report.

My friend and colleague David F. Aberle has contributed so much to my understanding of the ethnographic literature and of primitive societies that whatever may be sound in my interpretations will owe much to him. My research assistants, Albert Cafagna and David Kaplan, provided invaluable assessments of anthropological research along with their detailed reports about religion in certain primitive societies. Kathleen Gough Aberle, Wolfram Eberhard, Alfred Kroeber, Oscar Lewis, David Mandelbaum, Philip Rieff, Milton Singer, and Julian Steward were kind enough to give me needed information not contained in the published material concerning societies about which each has specialized knowledge. I have also benefited from the critical reading given an early draft of this manuscript by David Aberle, Robert Angell, Wolfram Eberhard, Morris Janowitz, David Mandelbaum, and Melford Spiro.

These pages are dedicated to L. G. Wayne Furman because he supplied me with their essential perspective: that religion is not just another name for economics, government, or the unconscious, and that religious beliefs are not mere fantasies.

G.E.S.

CONTENTS

CHAPTER I

THE SUPERNATURAL: ITS NATURE AND ORIGINS

Most men at most times have lived in two environments—one natural, the other supernatural. The distinction between these worlds is sometimes sharp, sometimes vague. It has even been declared an illusion. For the atheist, there are no gods—for the pantheist, all of nature is also supernatural.

The structure of the supernatural world, like that of the natural, varies greatly in human experience. It may have the august unity of Jehovah or teem with spirits and sprites, with gods and godlings, or with disembodied magical forces and ghosts. Toward man, the supernatural may be indifferent, spiteful, wantonly malevolent, supportive, supervisory, distant, intimate, transcendent, or immanent. Toward the supernatural, man may be scornful, friendly, fearful, awe-struck, manipulative, indifferent, submissive, reverent, joyful, aggressive, or loving.

The two worlds of nature and supernature confront us with innumerable mysteries. Of these, none seems more intricate than the discovery of human experiences which might give rise to a conception of this twofold character of the universe. Our understanding of behavior suggests that all ideas arise from man's experience with his surroundings. From what experiences do the ideas of the supernatural and its myriad forms arise? The studies to which we shall turn have this as their guiding question.

We shall find, however, that verifiable answers to so broad a question are almost impossible to obtain. It will be profitable, instead, to ask a number of narrower questions, each of which contributes toward solving the more general problem. We shall ask about the experiences from which seven ideas might originate: the conceptions of a monotheistic deity, of polytheistic gods, of ancestral spirits, reincarnation, the immanence of the soul, the prevalence of witchcraft, and the notion of gods who concern themselves with human moral problems. Our explanations for each of these beliefs will be tested against information from fifty primitive and ancient societies. In addition, we shall speculate about the conditions under which a disbelief in the supernatural comes into being.

Throughout these chapters we speak of experiences and beliefs. To avoid repetition, words such as "supernatural" or "reincarnation" or "monotheism" often appear without being labeled as beliefs or conceptions. This economy of expression is employed for its own merits, not to imply that any particular belief has literal validity.

A thorough and systematic treatment of a question such as ours cannot yet be written. The detailed evidence required does not exist. The elegantly clear and full explanations are not at hand. Yet some new explorations and advances are possible. There are certain roughhewn explanations which could not be tested until recently, when reliable information about the religions of many peoples became available. The purpose of this chapter is to describe and refine these pioneering explanations. Succeeding chapters offer some evidence about their validity.

CAN THE ORIGINS OF BELIEF IN THE
SUPERNATURAL BE DETERMINED?

It is often asserted that the question asked in these studies cannot be answered by any means known to science. If this were true, everything that we do here would be pointless. It is necessary, therefore, to say something about this assertion that our quest is hopeless.

We may begin by remembering that no procedure of empirical science allows us to determine with absolute certainty that one event, call it X, is the cause of another event, call it Y. Those who reject the possibility of studying the origin of beliefs in the supernatural usually insist on the absolute certainty which is never available in human knowledge of any subject. What one can sometimes show is that Y always appears after X is present and that Y appears only after X is present. We can never be certain that X and Y will have this relationship under all possible conditions because we are able to study them in only a limited number of situations. We can never be certain that it is X, as such, rather than some aspect of X or something which always accompanies X without being a part of it, which is the necessary and sufficient antecedent of Y. For many practical purposes, it may not be necessary to have such refined knowledge. All we may need to know is that by producing or preventing the appearance of X, we can control the appearance of Y.

Our confidence that X is the cause of Y is increased by several factors. We are more confident that a causal relation exists if we have some logically valid reasons for thinking that it should. Our confidence is also increased if the relationship appears under a wide variety of conditions, if alternative explanations can be discarded as contrary to empirical observations, and if we are able to control the appearance of antecedent conditions other than X so that X alone seems to precede Y.

Although the factors just listed increase one's confidence, they do not constitute a conclusive demonstration that X, as such, is always or ever the cause of Y. The working scientist seeks to establish causal relations which hold "for all practical purposes." He recognizes that conclusive demonstrations of causality are impossible.

Although absolute empirical proof of any positive assertion about causality is out of the question, absolute empirical disproof of such assertions is often quite possible. Investigators may show, for example, that Y appears in the absence of X or that X is not always followed by Y. It is a curious fact of human existence that we can be absolutely certain that something is not true, but only more or less certain that something is true.

The survey of leading explanations of the origin of supernature which we shall undertake will show that these accounts can usually be subjected to some empirical test. Many times we can demonstrate that an explanation is contrary to observations and so reject it. On other occasions we shall find that current evidence for an explanation is ambiguous, but that we can describe some feasible investigation which is likely to resolve the ambiguity. Finally, we shall discover at least one explanation which seems consistent with current knowledge and for which a variety of empirical tests are possible, thus providing us with a growing factual foundation for increasing or decreasing our confidence in the account. This survey indicates that the question of the supernatural's origin is one which can be investigated within the canons of empirical science.

We should, however, foresee two situations which limit studies of this topic. First, there are some explanations which call for unavailable information. These cannot be tested. Second, we cannot always find methods for ruling out the influence of factors which might provide alternative explanations to the account we advance. These limitations are not peculiar to the study of the supernatural's origins, but they are of importance in such investigations.

Two types of untestable explanations of supernatural beliefs are common. One of these asserts something about the experiences and inferences of prehistoric men. The other says that men developed their ideas of supernature by direct experiences with mana and spirits.

Since we have no records of how prehistoric men felt or reasoned, and no prospects of obtaining any, we cannot hope to verify hypotheses which depend on such evidence. As we shall see, however, we can occasionally show that explanations founded on assumptions about prehistory are improbable.

It is fortunate that we need not be troubled by our inability to test theories which depend on the unavailable evidence of prehistory. Our knowledge about beliefs shows that they do not persist by themselves. An idea or attitude or belief must correspond to current experiences with the environment if it is to continue across the generations. As a result, we may expect that forces which produce and support current beliefs are present along with those beliefs. What we do not know is whether the beliefs are now engendered by the same experiences which produced them in the past.

When, on the other hand, we are told that direct contacts with mana or spirits produced certain beliefs, we confront a different obstacle to verification. Because, by definition, these supernatural entities stand apart from the natural universe, freed of its laws and limitations, we are not able to observe them reliably through the instruments of nature. We cannot, for example, be certain that a spirit was or was not active in a particular situation. We cannot forecast with certainty that a spirit will take some course of action. We cannot say whether a magical spell is effective because, although unknown to us, someone's countermagic may be working against us. Such considerations make these accounts untestable by systematic empirical study.

THE EXPERIENCE OF THE SUPERNATURAL

How shall we tell the supernatural from the natural? Some answer must be given to this question before one can venture a guess about the experiences from which an idea of supernature originates.

Supernatural forces take one of two forms. There is what we shall call "mana" and there are spirits of various kinds.

Mana is a substance or essence which gives one the ability to perform tasks or achieve ends otherwise impossible. It increases natural abilities and confers supernatural skills. In itself, however, mana is an object, not a body of skills and abilities which are obtained through learning. Access to it is acquired, in the sense that a house or a wife or a spear are acquired, that is as a gift, as a purchase, or through the performance of appropriate acts.

When, for example, a Blackfoot Indian sought mana, he would go alone to some isolated spot. There, after fasting, prayer, and exposure to the elements, a spirit might come and teach him a song or dance or might tell him that he would find some plant or animal which would, thereafter, be a source of good luck. Returning to his band, the Indian would employ these gifts to bring success in love or in hunting, to improve his performance as a warrior, to heal the sick, or to aid in his other endeavors. It was common that he would incorporate objects of which the spirit told him into a medicine bundle, a convenient form in which to carry his talisman at all times. Such bundles could be purchased by those who lacked a spirit's visitation or who wanted to add to the charms which they owned. It is significant, however, that the spirits did not confer mana itself. Instead, they gave rituals or objects which enabled a man to make mana serve his needs.

Mana may be directed toward the achievement of the individual's purposes or those of a group. In either case, it is a substance which must be infused with human intentions or the intentions of spirits before its potentialities are realized. By itself, it does nothing. It is not able to organize events or to create them.

Spirits are supernatural beings. Unlike mana, they are personified. They have purposes and intentions of their own as well as the power to achieve their objectives.

Unfortunately for the construction of neat classifications, some personified supernatural forces fall between our categories of mana and spirit. Like mana they seem to have no objectives of their own, lying dormant until men activate them in the interest of human desires. At the same time, however, these forces are thought of as having the form of persons, animals, or other living creatures. We shall call them protospirits.

What makes mana, protospirits, and spirits supernatural? How, for example, does mana differ from a medical injection or a machine which enables men to do what formerly was impossible? How does the nature of spirits differ from that of unusually strong or capable people who can master problems which are unsolved by others? The anthropologist Malinowski [1] has taken great pains to show that primitives distinguish between the supernatural and other forces. Of what does that distinction consist?

Any answer to this question is speculative, but let us consider one which seems to fit the facts and which leads to interesting consequences. This answer says that behind natural events lies the supernatural—a realm of potentialities and purposes of which natural events are but concretions or expressions even as human behaviors or artifacts are expressions of the potentialities and purposes held by the men who produce them. [2] Let us suppose that mana represents the potentialities which underlie nature. Spirits represent organized clusters of the underlying purposes.

Now potentialities can serve a variety of purposes. In what is usually called magic, a person infuses mana with his own purposes. He activates the possibilities embodied in these transcendent conceptions, and thus influences the natural world by changing the supernatural. Spirits, representing purposes and possessing immediate access to the potentialities which underlie nature, can also manipulate natural events.

When he is confined to the world of nature, man is unable to produce what he wants merely by having the desire to do so, by informing the natural order with his purposes. Instead he must act upon it directly. He must create changes in the material universe which, of themselves, produce yet other changes until his objective is reached. At no point do his ideas or purposes, as such, intervene to change the environment. They must, in every case, be implemented by material action in the material world or that world remains as it was.

Supernatural forces are free of these limitations imposed on natural action in the material world. Many properties of the supernatural exemplify this freedom. A powerful spirit has but to desire rain and the waters fall. He can be at once in nature but not of it. Men will not perceive him directly through their senses. They will not find it inconsistent that he can be everywhere at once or that he can do many things at the same time. Not only do supernatural forces have powers not given to men, but, unless opposed by other and stronger spirits or by magic, the ends toward which those forces are directed are always accomplished. Finally, it is a common belief that the supernatural powers, unlike mankind, are immortal. They neither die nor become impotent with age.

These distinctions make it plain that we blur important differences in belief if we say that magic is only the science of primitives or that social movements like Fascism or Communism are of the same cloth as Christianity or Buddhism. There are similarities between magic and science. Both, for example, seek to understand and control nature. Likewise, both secular and religious movements may embody values which men seek with great devotion. But the underlying philosophy of science ignores the supernatural, and secular

creeds, as such, either ignore supernature or deny its existence. Magic and religion remain distinctive in having contacts with the supernatural as their goal.

ORIGINS OF EXPERIENCES OF THE SUPERNATURAL

But, from what human experiences do conceptions of
mana and spirit—of the supernatural—arise? As we examine
those explanations of the supernatural which locate its origin in experiences with nature, we find great diversity. We
shall consider a few of the more prestigious and plausible
notions from among this multitude of suggestions.[3]

In his famous survey of primitive religion, Lowie [4] expresses a conception which has wide support:

. . . Religion is verily a universal feature of human culture . . .
because all [societies] recognize in some form or other awe-
inspiring, extraordinary manifestations of reality. The present
treatise is accordingly dedicated to the discussion of those cultural phenomena of the simpler societies which center about
or are somehow connected with the sense of mystery or weird-
ness. . . .

There is no doubt that men often explain the strange
and awe-inspiring as expressions of the supernatural. But,
as it stands, Lowie's account falls short of explaining certain
facts. For example, it does not tell us why some primitive
peoples seem to lack religious explanations of nature's more
spectacular features, while explaining many ordinary and
mundane events as the work of the spirits. Second, it does
not show why all men or some men should inevitably attribute a supernatural origin to puzzling or unusual events.

After all, whether among primitives or among ourselves, we find a variety of reactions to mysterious happenings. Sometimes people just admit to uncertainty and wonderment. Sometimes they propose natural explanations. Sometimes they try to investigate the possible natural causes behind the unusual. There is nothing in Lowie's notion that allows us to say which of these responses will occur. Lowie certainly does not demonstrate that mystification must lead men to develop conceptions of mana or spirit and, subsequently, to employ these conceptions as explanations of the mysterious.

The second objection to Lowie's scheme is particularly important because it applies to a number of other efforts to explain the rise of supernatural beliefs. It is relevant, for example, to the notion that theologies are comforting rationales which men develop to make life bearable—to compensate for fears and frustrations and unfulfilled desires. The supernatural is said to be a gigantic fulfillment of dreams which people cannot realize in nature. Or, we are told, people feel more secure if they have some explanation of the difficulties they encounter in life, and religious ideas arise to provide this explanation.

We may have hesitations about accepting the notion that supernatural beliefs are only pleasant compensatory myths. We may wonder why, if men can make any fantasy they choose, some primitive peoples picture the afterlife as a gray, uninteresting existence or why the traditional Christian concerns himself with a hell or why many peoples populate the world with demons. Whatever we conclude about such problems, we can be certain that there are many ways in which men respond to fear, failure, and insecurity, and that, by themselves, disquieting experiences and unresolved difficulties do not force the development of supernatural explanations.

Is a belief in the supernatural a consequence of ignorance about the empirical world and the possibility of explaining that world in natural terms? Does the need for a concept of supernature disappear to the extent that firm empirical understanding advances? This can be a most involved question from some approaches, but it may be resolved rather simply for our purposes by the device of turning it around. Does a lack of such empirical understanding force upon man a conception of supernature? Clearly, the absence of some experience is not, in itself, sufficient to provide another experience. At best then, the argument that beliefs in supernature decline with an increase in empirical understanding might explain the rise of atheism, but the inverse of this argument surely does not explain the presence of religion or magic. And this leaves us with our original problem of locating the experiences which lead to a conception of mana and spirit.

That gifted pioneer in anthropology, Edward Tylor,[5] proposed that the nature of life, of sleep, of death, and of dreams was the stuff which inspired religious thought. Reflecting on these mysteries, man, Tylor suggested, developed the distinction between the human body and the spirit dwelling within it. Then, having evolved the concept of a soul, people proceeded to generalize their new idea from themselves to other natural phenomena. The "souls" of nations and of such important climatic conditions as the sunshine and rain are what we know as the higher deities of polytheism. These souls differ in rank, but not in character, from the souls of men.

. . . It seems as though the conception of a human soul . . . served as a type or model on which [man] framed not only his ideas of other souls of lower grade, but also his ideas of spiritual beings in general, from the tiniest elf that sports in the long grass up to the heavenly Creator and Ruler of the world, the Great Spirit (p. 196).

What led men to generalize the idea of soul in this manner? Tylor answered:

. . . Spirits are simply personified causes. As men's ordinary life and actions were held to be caused by souls, so the happy or disastrous events which affect mankind, as well as the manifold physical operations of the outer-world, were accounted for as caused by soul-like beings . . . (pp. 194–95).

Once more we can be certain that we do not have the whole story. Tylor tells us nothing of why some of the simpler peoples connect dreams with supernatural events while others do not. Nor do we find, as he believes, that primitives universally attribute all otherwise unexplained events to the actions of spirits. Perhaps our anthropologists have not probed these matters with enough persistence and skill. From present evidence, however, we cannot find the universal beliefs in these matters which Tylor suggests should exist. Finally, we may observe that Tylor's account is one of those which requires unobtainable information about man's prehistoric inferences. This requirement makes it untestable.

Each explanation of religion which has just been reviewed has its more sophisticated versions and each has, on occasion, been combined with others to produce a more complete account. It would be tedious indeed to recapitulate all of them. It is also unnecessary. We have found that each fails to explain why men experience some parts of the universe as having the properties of mana and why they should attribute some events to the actions of beings having the properties of spirits—personality, intentions, immortality, invisibility, freedom from nature's restrictions, and the rest. An adequate account must explain all these features of supernature. It is not enough to say that men are fearful or mystified or that they are ignorant of nature's laws. These experiences might send people in search of relief and reassurance, but they do not determine that men will develop notions of spirit and mana. The older explanations do not lack all merit. They are not completely out of touch with the facts of supernatural experiences. It is what they fail to do, not what they accomplish, that needs attention if we wish to grow beyond them.

The most elaborate attempt to confront the contents of supernatural experiences and construct a theory adequate to them is that of a French sociologist, Emile Durkheim.[6] His approach is through an analysis of religious beliefs.

All known religious beliefs, whether simple or complex, present one common characteristic: they presuppose a classification of all things, real and ideal, of which men think, into two classes or opposed groups, generally designated by two distinct terms which are translated well enough by the words *profane* and *sacred*. This division of the world into two domains, the one containing all that is sacred, the other all that is profane, is the distinctive trait of religious thought. . . .

Parsons [7] offers an admirable summary of Durkheim's reasoning from this distinction.

. . . Directly contrasting the attitudes appropriate in a . . . [sacred] context with those towards objects of utilitarian significance and their use in fields of rational technique, he found one fundamental feature of the sacred to be its radical dissociation from any utilitarian context. The sacred is to be treated with a certain specific attitude of respect, which Durkheim identified with the appropriate attitude toward moral obligations and authority. . . .

The central significance of the sacred in religion, however, served to raise in a peculiarly acute form the question of the source of the attitude of respect. . . . Durkheim opened up an entirely new line of thought by suggesting that . . . [there] was in fact no common intrinsic quality of things treated as sacred which could account for the attitude of respect. In fact, almost everything from the sublime to the ridiculous has in some society been treated as sacred. Hence the source of sacredness is not intrinsic; the problem is of a different character. Sacred objects and entities are symbols. The problem then becomes one of identifying the referents of such symbols. . . .

At this point Durkheim became aware of the fundamental significance of his previous insight that the attitude of respect for sacred things was essentially identical with the attitude of respect for moral authority. If sacred things are symbols, the essential quality of that which they symbolize is that it is an entity which would command moral respect. It was by this path that Durkheim arrived at the famous proposition that society is always the real object of religious veneration. . . .

How can men's experience of their society produce the concept of supernature? Because, says Durkheim, the relation of men to their society is like that of the worshipper to his god. Like the spirits, societies dominate their members by so controlling their thoughts and desires that individuals find intangible forces within themselves directing their conduct. Second, men feel strong, confident, and at peace with themselves when fulfilling their society's mandates. Third, as Lowie [8] puts it, "all of a man's cultural possessions are the gift of society." Society and culture go on though particular individuals perish. They provide an environment of directives and skills and values which persist in seeming perpetuity. And, Lowie continues to summarize:

In short, the individual consciousness finds an environment peopled with forces at once transcendentally potent and helpful, august yet benevolent; it objectifies its relevant impressions as we objectify our sensations, but with a significant difference: these sensations do not evoke the sentiment of awe, they correspond to the profane as contrasted with the sacred part of the universe. . . .

Whatever the flaws in Durkheim's thought, and they exist,[9] it has the exceptional merit of directing our attention to a possibility quite in keeping with the character of supernature. It suggests that men develop a concept of personified supernatural beings directly from the model which their society provides. Unaware, as they generally are, of the extent to which overt behavior and inner impulse are formed by relations with other people, men find themselves in the hands of mysterious forces. Unlike other forces, these social customs seem to speak to individuals, chiding them for misbehavior, directing them to choose some goals rather than others, and rewarding their conformity. The thoroughly socialized individual has so acquired these social standards that they are effective in directing his conduct even when he is quite alone.

And, we might add to Durkheim's discussion, unlike the law of the lever, or the principle of gravitation or other conditions of the physical world, these inner forces bear directly on a man's motives. They can be interested in what he intended as well as what he did.

Durkheim's position is plausible just because it begins to explain why men come to know intangible forces which can enter human lives, controlling will and action, and why these are forces with which people must come to terms. But much is left to be desired.

First, Durkheim's scheme does not suggest how spirits come to be unified and personified beings. Why should they not be experienced as powerful but disconnected impulses?

Second, what is the society that is venerated? Is it the composite of all the effects which contacts with one another have on people's conduct? Is it the pattern of such contacts? Is it but one special kind of social relationship to which people may belong? If there are gods of the winds or sea or the heavenly bodies, how can these somehow be the society in other guise when human actions do not exert obvious control over these natural forces? Is it all of the society that is venerated or just some of its aspects? Certainly the state or the economy or educational institutions are not considered supernatural in character by modern societies and we can find many primitive counterparts for this judgment.

Third, all spirits are not respected or venerated. Demons and devils may be feared, but they are not objects of moral respect. Other spirits are ignored or ridiculed or punished by those who believe in their existence. A satisfactory theory of supernatural beliefs must account for those relations between men and their gods. Durkheim's scheme does not provide the necessary explanation.

What I propose is to give tentative acceptance to the spirit, if not to the details, of Durkheim's position. I shall assume that some experiences with other people generate the concept of supernature and its two forms—mana and spirit. From that point, however, one must take a speculative path toward a more complete and plausible account than Durkheim provides. It begins with a reconsideration of the nature of the supernatural, especially of spirits, and, after suggesting social experiences capable of producing a notion of personified supernatural beings, proceeds to extend the interpretation to include the presence of mana. This interpretation provides predictions which are tested in later chapters.

THE ORIGIN OF SPIRITS

Spirits, we have seen, are organized clusters of purposes, each having a personal identity and access to mana. They are immortal. They may be invisible. They usually maintain their abilities through the years, not becoming feeble through age or illness. Only the powers of other supernatural beings limit the exercise of their skills. If we accept Durkheim's judgment that social experiences are the most likely source of supernatural concepts, to what social relationships do the experiences of spirits correspond?

Men may experience purpose in the acts of individuals or groups. That is, they find the behavior of individuals and groups directed toward goals, and learn that present conduct is shaped to promote the accomplishment of objectives. Purposes are the ideas people hold of what they will try to obtain in the future—a home, a lover, success in hunting, wealth, prestige, rectitude, or whatever.

It happens, however, that people may have unintended effects on one another and that some influences they desire to wield are, nevertheless, denied them. Thus the exercise of purpose is not always clearly and cleanly seen as related to the consequences people have for each other's behavior. This fact has important implications for our work. If spirits are purposing beings, their influences flowing from their intentions, then we may expect that the social relations corresponding to supernatural beings must be those in which the connection of intention and effect is evident.

But we can say more. The spirits are immortal. More accurately, their life span is greater than that of man. This qualification is entered because ancestors may take the form of spirits, at least in the thought of a generation or two of their descendants. It may be, however, that the dead sometimes cease to be considered as spirits once their names and deeds are lost to living memory. When the purposes—the spirit—of an individual or group persist although the individual dies or the group's membership undergoes complete change, one must assume that those purposes continue to be embodied and active in survivors. Thus, when we seek the origin of spirits, we shall look for social relationships regarded as persisting across the generations. Individuals come and go. Groups may persist.

A further clue in our search is found in the fact that spirits have an identity. This does not mean that they are always named or that the peculiar traits of a particular spirit are invariably given a full and distinctive portrayal. It does mean that the notion of a spirit involves a particular and organized entity. The gods are individuals, not diffuse conditions. This fact suggests that we should look for *particular* groups as the source of the concept of spirit.

Finally, where there are several spirits, their purposes differ in some respects. They may protect different families or govern diverse aspects of nature or seek peculiar forms of attention from men and one another. These differences imply that we should search for groups with distinctive purposes.

To summarize, the characteristics of spirits suggest that we identify them with specific groups which persist over time and have distinctive purposes. What groups meet these specifications? Our next step is to propose an answer to this question.

There is a term in law and political science which seems to catch the qualities we seek. It is "sovereignty." A group has sovereignty to the extent that it has original and independent jurisdiction over some sphere of life—that its power to make decisions in this sphere is not delegated from outside but originates within it, and that its exercise of this power cannot legitimately be abrogated by another group. Although the term "sovereignty" is commonly applied to nations or states, it can be applied to other groups as well.

In the United States, as in most societies, the family is a sovereign group. It has original and independent jurisdiction, within certain limits, over such matters as the education of the children, the practice of religion, the use of leisure, and the choice of goods to be purchased. Similarly, among Americans, the national state has sovereignty over certain areas of importance, as have the several states, the counties, townships, local communities, and other organizations.[10] In one society or another, clans, chiefdoms, extended families, and many other types of organizations will be found to meet the criteria which identify a sovereign group.

To make the point still clearer, we may consider organizations which do not have sovereignty. These usually will include the armed forces, the schools, and other agencies which are but specialized arms of sovereign groups, their purposes dictated by the organizations which have sovereignty and their powers delegated to them for the accomplishment of such purposes. We shall also include under this heading of nonsovereign, all groups devoted primarily to ritual or ceremonial functions, for the events they celebrate and symbolize are typically those of other agencies. Religious bodies would be in this category in most primitive societies, perhaps in all societies. The classification of religious groups is a problem to which we shall give further attention in a later chapter.

In these studies, we shall assume that insofar as a group has sovereignty, it is likely [11] to provide the conditions from which a concept of spirit originates. The purposes of sovereign groups, like their special spheres of influence, tend to be distinctive and clear. By contrast, the purposes of nonsovereign groups are more likely to be seen as coming from a source other than themselves. The identity of the sovereign group is especially clear-cut just because its areas of control, and hence its purposes, are readily located. All we need add is the requirement that such a group shall persist over time. This will almost certainly be the case for many groups in any stable and enduring society.

Nevertheless, a critic would be right in saying that these groups, as such, are not worshipped or venerated as supernatural. What features are associated with them that provoke the notion of supernature? The speculative solution of this problem is founded on some further observations about groups.

THE ORIGIN OF SUPERNATURE

The argument to be outlined here states that people experience "supernatural" properties in social life not merely because men are unwittingly controlled by social norms which they learn, but because social relationships inherently possess the characteristics we identify as supernatural. This argument is clearer if we let it flow from an illustration. Let us consider, therefore, the origin and organization of a particular social relationship, a marriage, and let us suppose that we deal with the American case.

As in any voluntary relationship, the partners to a marriage join together because they facilitate one another's realization of objectives. I mean to imply that these considerations account for the union's existence whether the parties concerned know it or not. In the case of a marriage, one presumes that the partners enable each other to reach such goals as the rearing of children, achievement of status as full adults in the eyes of the community, the mutual exploration and development of their personalities, economic support, sexual satisfaction, and, in some cases, a strengthening of the families from which they come.

In their first contacts, the individuals learn whether they can find such satisfactions in each other. They discover the kinds of relationships which best satisfy their needs. If a suitable form of interaction does develop, the man and woman, who first committed themselves only to exploration, now prepare to commit enough of such resources as affection, time, and economic skills to maintain the relationship. In our example, we may think of dating before marriage as a period of exploration and of courtship as an extended

period for completing the exploration and developing a
stable relationship once preliminary investigation brings
promising results. At some point in this process, the couple
must commit themselves to perform such acts as will make
possible the continuing satisfaction of their desires or the
marriage will not exist other than in name.

What is being described is the emergence of a pattern of
interaction between people, an exchange of desired behaviors, which can be used to reach certain goals and which
is a prerequisite to such an accomplishment. This pattern
incorporates an arrangement by which participants perform
certain services for each other and, in return, receive services
they desire. Presumably certain minimal arrangements of
this kind are required for any relationship to persist. Once
in existence, to return to the marital illustration, they allow
the couple to work together in bearing and rearing children,
entertaining guests, managing the economic affairs of a
household, and in endless other activities.

These underlying and requisite arrangements may be
called the "constitutional arrangements" or "constitutional
structure" of the relationship. The constitutional arrangements "define" those affairs with which the organization
may legitimately concern itself and the procedures by which
its activities may legitimately be formulated and implemented. To put the matter a bit differently, constitutional
arrangements "state" a group's sphere of competence and
the proper procedures for making and executing decisions.
The words "define" and "state" are put in quotation marks
to indicate that the achievement of a constitutional structure
and the perception of its nature may or may not be self-
conscious and symbolized in the experience of the partic-

ipants. On occasion, as in the Constitution of the United States, some of the arrangements' more important features are given express statement. Similarly, the marriage vows make overt a part of those arrangements requisite to establishing a family. But it is typical that all features of the constitutional structure are not made explicit and, in such groupings as friendships, it may be that none of these features is symbolized.

How, then, do we know that constitutional arrangements exist? Locke, Hume, Rousseau and others invented historical episodes in which men first came together and, explicitly acknowledging their interdependence and the conditions under which they would live together, founded societies. Something like these fictive situations actually occurs at constitutional conventions or when articles of incorporation are drawn up and signed. But when is the constitutional structure of a marriage apparent? Of a friendship? Of a new sectarian movement?

The presence of certain minimal conditions under which an organization can continue in existence will come to light when there is a likelihood that such conditions will not be met. These are the constitutional problems of a marriage or a nation or of any other organization. The "constitution" need not be written in order for the problems to exist and be recognized precisely as those which affect the group's continuation. Thus, a man and wife who cannot conceive of marriage to a person who is sexually unfaithful must revise the constitutional structure governing their relations or sever those relations if one of them is discovered having an extramarital affair.

It is the mark of a stable and legitimate [12] social relationship that the constitutional structure is consistent with the secondary, tertiary, and other successive relations which are built on it. Only on rare occasions, furthermore, is it necessary in such a relationship to refer self-consciously to the constitutional structure itself to decide an issue. The operations which that structure permits are visible, not the constitutional structure itself. Constant examination by participants of their basic commitments to each other suggests that the foundations of the relationship are unstable. It is the nature of reform to debate the application of the constitutional structure, not its character. Revolution debates the validity of the constitutional structure itself.

Before relating all these observations to the concept of supernature, let us explore just a bit further the fact that not all aspects of a constitutional structure are made explicit and symbolic. This can be important in understanding the nature of mana and spirits.

We have seen that the constitutional structure, itself, emerges from the many interests and desires of the participants in a relationship. It expresses, implicitly or overtly, their minimal demands on one another if their interaction is to continue. But some interests and desires which lead to such demands go forever unrecognized. Others become more or less apparent as the relationship continues. And close inspection would probably show that every taste and attitude and intention of the participants has some bearing, however distant, on the constitutional structure of every particular relationship in which it is involved. This vast, largely uncharted and unchartable body of dispositions and potentialities which each participant brings to a given relationship, and which changes with new experiences, provides the primordial conditions from which specific constitutional arrangements emerge.

The constitutional structure of a social relationship is like the notion of "character" [13] in the individual. Despite the considerable differences in a person's behavior from one situation to another, we recognize certain attitudes and values as somehow enduring in his conduct and central to it. These predispositions have to do with the goals and means to which he is most thoroughly committed—those habits for whose maintenance he will pay the highest price. He need not be self-consciously aware of all or any such predispositions. Indeed, he typically is unaware of most of them. Yet they manifest themselves rather clearly when their existence is challenged and they provide a continuing, if subterranean, set of forces which orders many of his activities. As with a group's constitutional structures, these basic features of a person's identity are relatively organized areas of predispositions toward the environment, and are surrounded by tastes and desires which have been subjected to less searching evaluation from experiences in the environment. Such terms as Freud's "primary process" have been used to refer to this analogue in the individual of what, in social life, we have called the primordial.[14]

But how is all of this related to the supernatural? Let me suggest that the primordial links among men—vague, largely hidden, possessing unsuspected potentialities—correspond to the idea that the world is the expression or concretion of latent possibilities which, when infused with appropriate purposes, can be combined or rearranged or activated to serve human needs. This is the stuff that magic seeks to manipulate. By contrast, constitutional structures, and especially those of sovereign groups, are areas of partially organized and orderly influence in this primordial ocean. They represent the crystallization of purposes which spring from the nature of the primordial and whose consequences flow back into it. These constitutional structures are what men often conceptualize as personified and supernatural beings. Religion consists of behaviors directed toward influencing the purposes of such beings—of spirits.[15]

Both the primordial and the constitutional structures in which human life is immersed have properties which are also those that define the supernatural. As conditions which underlie the flow of conscious experience and interaction, they are immanent in their guidance of the particular experiences of any given moment, yet transcendent in the continuity of their influence over many different experiences. Like relations in supernature, the relations within and between the primordial and constitutional structures are largely invisible and their effects are accomplished through the directives and limitations they set out for the conceptions of people who interact.

The influence of these structures upon participants in interaction is also like the supernatural in possessing powers not given to men. Their influence operates at all times. Without the application of any obvious or perceptible means, these structures determine people's relations and activities—both generating them and judging them. Further, these structures embody a wider "knowledge" than any individual or group possesses in the sense that they contain more conditions and potentialities than those of which people are aware at any given time. The accomplishment of their purposes is inevitable as long as they are stable, for the only contingency required for that accomplishment is the presence of normal, well-socialized humans who are committed to the relationships which these structures undergird. They cannot, of course, be avoided or escaped by such humans. Here, then, we have entities which are not perceived in any direct sense, which may have some empirical site as their locale but not as their being, which have powers that transcend the means-ends processes of nature, which can affect nature without being of it, and which may or may not be experienced as having an enduring identity.

Any given social organization or group consists of a constitutional structure together with the interrelations among participants which that structure permits and directs. Such interrelations are an organization of activities for implementing and maintaining the constitutional structure. This has been illustrated in the example of a marriage.

Drawing together the pieces of this explanation of the supernatural we may conclude:

1. The experiences which seem closest to having the supernatural's characteristics are those connected with the primordial and constitutional structures of social relationships.

a. Like the supernatural, these structures embody purposes. They also embody those potentialities which can be put to work for beings who can infuse them with purpose.

b. Like the supernatural, these structures pervade the inner life and outer experience of men, directing and limiting human behavior as invisible, immortal, inescapable, and vaguely understood forces whose effects on conduct seem to be produced by the direct induction of purpose.

2. The conception of spirits corresponds to experiences with the activities of sovereign organizations. More pre-

cisely, the spirits whom men approach do not represent particular sovereign organizations, as such, but their constitutional structures. Spirits stand for the complex and vaguely bounded constitutional structures which are given partial concretion in particular sovereign organizations and which exhibit consistencies and continuities of operation while always escaping complete and explicit embodiment in any human group.[16] Spirits are likely to represent sovereign groups rather than other types of social organization because the purposes and spheres of influence of such groups, and hence of their constitutional structures, are more clearly available to the experience of participants.

3. The idea of mana is evoked by experiences with the primordial features of social life.

4. For our purposes, magic will consist of those behaviors designed to invest mana with a particular purpose; religion, of activities aimed at influencing, or responding to, the purposes of spirits.

Like other explanations this account of the supernatural will doubtlessly be shown to contain flaws. It is certain that it rests on many assumptions for which current evidence is inadequate. In any event, its value lies in its ability to organize facts which other schemes cannot interpret and, going further, to explain observations which cannot be integrated by alternative interpretations. Its value is further enhanced if it leads one to make verifiable predictions and if such verification is forthcoming. Attempts to make and test such predictions provide the contents for the chapters which follow.

These speculative notions will be applied to a wide variety of theological ideas, testing to see if our theory leads us to social conditions with which the theologies are associated. Specifically, we shall search for the social roots of monotheism, polytheism, ancestor worship, reincarnation, highly prevalent witchcraft, the identification of the individual's soul with his body, and the support of human moral codes by the spirits. These theological beliefs were selected for study because information concerning them was available, and available in considerable detail. By contrast, a number of supernatural conditions were often too sparsely described to permit investigation. These included the existence of spirits attached to particular places or objects, demons, and minor sprites, elves, fairies, and the like. Some means may later be found for employing even these scant materials. We shall, of course, be especially interested to learn whether all of the types of spirits we study have in common an association with certain social conditions. In this chapter we reviewed the features of spirithood shared by all supernatural beings. We also suggested one pattern of social relations from which these features might spring. An important test of our theory's value is its ability to define correctly this one particular set of social relations which accompanies all manifestations of a belief in spirits.

We shall find, in Chapter X, that our seven theological beliefs tend to occur quite independently of one another in the primitive societies we study. This means that to know that a society has any one of them does not usually allow us to predict which of the rest are also present. Similarly, we shall find that the social indices related to each theological idea tend to occur independently of the social indices associated with any of the others.

In Chapter X we shall return to the speculative interpretation of the supernatural given here. We can then evaluate it against the findings from our studies and against its ability to explain the appearance of atheism. This procedure will not provide a full evaluation of the scheme's validity. We can say, however, that the tests provided are among those which a valid interpretation should meet and can judge whether other existing interpretations would be more adequate in this respect than our own.

CONCLUSION

In this chapter, we have examined the concepts of the supernatural world and its two common forms—mana and spirit. We have given speculative identification to certain characteristics of social life which seem to correspond to these concepts. In particular, we have considered primordial and constitutional structures as sources of the ideas of supernature, mana, and spirit. Succeeding chapters employ these ideas to explain such beliefs as monotheism, polytheism, reincarnation, and the prevalence of witchcraft.

We do not claim that the conditions outlined in this introduction are solely responsible for the beliefs discussed in later chapters. Such a statement is inherently untestable, for it implies that one shall consider all possible alternative explanations. Further, although we were able to show that many explanations of supernatural experiences were incomplete, we could not often reject one of them as utterly irrelevant. What will be urged is that the social conditions sketched in our theory, or factors related to them, may be important sources of a number of beliefs about the supernatural.[17]

CHAPTER II

METHODS OF STUDY

Before we can elaborate and test a variety of implications which flow from the ideas presented in Chapter I, we must find some way of relating those ideas to observations of nature. Certain methods of study find a place in all or several of the chapters which follow. They are described here. Other methods were devised for one particular problem and will be reported when that problem is discussed.

THE SAMPLE

The data for our work will come from observations of primitive and ancient peoples. There are at least two reasons for this choice. First, each of these peoples is likely to possess rather homogeneous beliefs about the supernatural world. By contrast, in a complex society such as the United States, we find wide differences in the conception of supernature. The absence of such differences simplifies our efforts to predict and understand. Second, the volume of important literature written about any complex society is so great that it takes a long time to examine it and a specialist's knowledge to evaluate and organize it. Again, tests of implications are easier to make when one deals with less elaborate societies.

Murdock has estimated [1] that something like 3,500 known

societies have existed on the earth. Since all of these cannot be studied, one must draw from among them a smaller number which, it is hoped, represents the 3,500. But there are problems in obtaining such a sample.

Some of these societies are quite like their neighbors in social organization and general culture. Such similarities frequently represent the heavy borrowing of cultural items by neighboring societies. On occasion, cultural similarities appear because two societies were originally one and the same. Should a large number of such related societies fall in one's sample, there would be serious reason to question the independence of the cases.

There is no thoroughly adequate way to eliminate these cross-cultural influences among the societies drawn in a sample, but Murdock provides an approximation. He has drawn up a list of some 556 societies [2] which contains no more than a few societies from each of these clusters of similar and neighboring peoples. The 556 cases are grouped into 50 broad regions of the world. A smaller sample may then be drawn from these cases.

But our problems do not end at this point. The descriptions of the 556 societies vary considerably in quality and completeness. Further, observations for a particular society may be excellent on some topic, say child rearing, and inaccurate or scant on another, say religious beliefs. For reasons which become apparent as we go along, tests of implications from our conception of the supernatural require a fairly complete description of a society's major institutions together with certain specific data about its beliefs in the supernatural.

A statement of the problem of these studies and a copy

of Murdock's list were presented to colleagues in anthropology [3] who specialize in various areas of the world. They were asked to indicate those societies in their area of specialization for which the needed information was likely to be available. These colleagues were also requested to indicate which of the societies they mentioned had been converted to one of the great world religions—Judaism, Christianity, Mohammedanism, Buddhism, and Hinduism—to such an extent that beliefs which might have sprung up in the society were obliterated. The objective was to avoid cases in which local conditions might not have generated the prevailing conceptions of the supernatural. Ancient Israel remained in the sample because Judaism was an indigenous product.

The rest of the procedure was simple. Each of Murdock's 556 societies for which suitable information could be had was given a number. One such society was then chosen at random from those in each of the 50 world regions into which Murdock divides his list. In the case of three regions, the Atlantic and Central Sudan areas of Africa and the Caucasian area, no societies could be selected either because none had been described in the manner required by the plan of this research or because all were heavily indoctrinated by one of the major world religions. Replacements were chosen at random from the remaining 47 regions.

The 50 societies listed below were selected in the fashion just described:

Region	Society
Oceania	
Polynesia	Marquesan
Micronesia	Ifaluk

Region	Society
Oceania (*continued*)	
Melanesia	Dobu
New Guinea	Arapesh, Orokaiva
Australia	Arunta
Indonesia	Iban
Philippines	Ifugao
Indian Ocean	Tanala (Menabe)
Africa	
Cape	Hottentot
Southeast Africa	Zulu (after King Shaka)
Southwest Africa	Lozi
Congo-Zambesi	Bemba
Tanganyika	Nyakyusa
Lake Region	Ganda
Equitoria	Azande
Guinea Coast	Ga (Temma)
Atlantic	none
Western Sudan	Tallensi
Plateau	Tiv
Central Sudan	none
Upper Nile	Nuer
Eastern Horn	Nandi
North Africa	Ancient Egyptians (Middle Kingdom)
Eurasia	
Europe	Romans (Age of Augustus)
Caucasia	none
Near East	Israelites (Era of the Judges)
Greater India	Toda
Southeast Asia	Karen (hill tribes)
East Asia	Miao (Ch'uan Miao)
Central Asia	Lepcha
Arctic Eurasia	Samoyed
North America	
Arctic America	Copper Eskimo
Subarctic America	Carrier, Kaska
Northwest Coast	Yurok

Region	Society
North America (*continued*)	
California	Pomo (northern groups)
	Yokuts
Great Basin	Shoshoni (Basin-plateau groups)
Plateau	Nez Percés
Plains	Blackfoot (post-horse)
Prairie	Winnebago
Eastern Woodlands	Iroquois (Seneca)
Southwest	Zuni
Mexico	Aztec
South America	
Circum-Caribbean	Cuna
Andes	Aymara
Amazonia	Yagua
Guiana	Carib
Eastern Brazil	Timbira
Mato Grosso	Trumai
Gran Chaco	Lengua
Patagonia	Yahgan

The parenthetical notes after the names of certain societies reflect another problem of sampling. In many places, there are several distinct groups with the same name, but organizationally unrelated to one another. Thus, among the Karen tribes of Burma, there are great cultural differences between those groups which practice dry rice cultivation in the hills and the Karen who live on the plains below. Again, as among the Ga towns of the West African coast, there are cultural differences due to varying contact with Europeans. Finally, as among the Egyptians or Israelites or Blackfoot, substantial variations in culture are reported between different historical periods. In each of these cases, one must select one group or one period of time as his referent.

Where the problem was one of choosing among subgroups differing in degree of contact with Western civilization, the choice was always that of the group having the least contact. When the choice was among various groups having different but equally indigenous cultures or among various periods of a society's history, the selection was made by numbering the groups or periods and picking one with the aid of a table of random numbers.

Our knowledge of many societies is founded on studies of one or a few communities in that society. Consultation of the Selected Bibliography at the end of this book will provide interested readers with a still more exact idea of the sources of information employed.

One certainly cannot say that the 50 peoples chosen are representative of all the simpler societies or of Murdock's list of 556. We can say that they represent a wide range of the world's simpler peoples, that some of the lack of independence produced among the sample's members by their borrowing from neighbor societies has been removed, that they are not concentrated in one or a few geographic regions, and that the method by which they were chosen was not knowingly biased in favor of the hypotheses we shall test in later chapters.

GATHERING INFORMATION

Once these 50 peoples were chosen, the objective was to read the principal descriptions available for each and to record pertinent data. Two advanced graduate students in anthropology [4] assisted in this work. Each of them read the materials on 13 societies. I covered the references for the remaining 24. Each of us followed the "Directions for Recording" which appear in Appendix I. Those Directions, developed after reading the monographs on a few societies not included in the sample, were designed to obtain a picture of the history and major institutions of each society in addition to certain specific information.

On another matter, we have adopted the decision of Zelditch.[5]

. . . it was taken as a policy decision . . . that all ethnographic reports would be accepted as accurate. This is not "epistemological realism," it is merely that to question one is to question all. It is for this reason, in fact, that a crude analysis depending for its significance primarily on replication was made at all.

DEFINING SOME INDICATORS

The notion of sovereign groups was presented in Chapter I and will be used many times in succeeding chapters. The rules for deciding which groups are sovereign, together with the rules for recognizing certain other social conditions which receive frequent mention in this report, will now be presented to simplify the exposition in the chapters which follow.

The indicators described in this section fall into three categories. First there are those which define sovereign and nonsovereign organizations. Second, there are a large number of indices referring to the complexity, specialization, and wealth of a society. Such indices tell us something of the setting in which sovereign groups function and something of their inner structure. Both considerations will assist our effort to relate sovereignty to the presence of spirits. The indicators in this second group record the following observations: the number of specialties in communal activities and noncommunal activities, the principal source of food, the amount of food produced, the amount of the bride price, the presence of debts, the existence of social classes, the presence of individually owned property, the nature of the local units in which the population is settled, and the size of the population of the ultimately sovereign organization. Third, and finally, there is an index of one kind of danger to which a society may be exposed: the degree of threat from armed attacks by alien peoples.

Two of these indicators, the amount of the bride price and the danger of attack by alien peoples, proved unreliable (see Appendix III). They are mentioned in this chapter simply to present a complete list of the classifications attempted, but they will play no further part in our work.

Some readers may wish only to skim the detailed definitions of the several indices, picking up just enough information to understand the essential points in each. There are, however, two considerations necessary for an understanding and evaluation of these indicators and the findings in later chapters.

The first such consideration has to do with the reliability with which information coded in these indices was abstracted from the records prepared by those of us who read the ethnographic reports. All coding was done by the author. When the "Directions for Recording" were compiled, the hypotheses discussed in the chapters on monotheism and ethical sanctions (Chapters III and IX) had been developed. The Directions asked for information relevant to a test of those hypotheses. While recording such information, readers were instructed to report other data on beliefs about the supernatural. It was not until after these reports were in hand, and after the data contained in them had been categorized, that the idea arose of extending the theory to account for polytheism, ancestor worship and the other topics treated in these chapters. No additional codes and classifications were constructed for these extensions.

It is important to face certain questions raised by these procedures. Since one of the three readers, the author, knew the hypotheses that were being tested, is it possible that he saw what he expected to find as he read the monographs, distorting the true contents of the ethnographers' reports? Since the author did all the categorizing of information abstracted from the monographs, would another person, and one who did not have foreknowledge of the hypotheses to be tested, obtain similar classifications? In short, would the procedures produce results biased in favor of the hypotheses?

The following considerations are relevant for an evaluation of these questions:

1. Some months after the first three readers had finished their reports and information from those reports had been categorized, sufficient funds became available [6] to employ two additional persons [7] to check on the results originally obtained. These new readers, advanced graduate students in anthropology, were not acquainted with our hypotheses. They read the monographic literature originally surveyed for 20 randomly selected societies chosen from the 50 societies in our sample. They then employed the codes originally used for categorizing the reports of the first three readers. A comparison of their coding with that done originally shows a satisfactory degree of agreement between

the two. These findings are reported in detail in Appendix III.

2. Appendix III also contains a comparison of certain codes originally prepared for this study with codes for the same material reported later by Murdock.[8] Once again there is a satisfactory degree of correspondence between the two independent classifications.

Although these studies of the reliability of our coding suggest that it is adequate, we regret that this work on reliability could not be done before the data were analyzed. Sufficient funds for that purpose were not then available or in prospect.

3. In any case, the author's reading and coding were not biased by a knowledge of the hypotheses reported in Chapters IV through VIII. Those hypotheses did not emerge until some time after the code was complete. We cannot, of course, rule out the possibility that the author's development of these latter hypotheses was influenced by his experience in coding. All that can be reported is that such influence seems unlikely given the lengthy and involved thought required to develop these hypotheses.

4. Finally, most of the observations classified under our indicators are such that there is minimal opportunity for a coder's biases to enter his work. For example, the ethnographer typically supplies us with a clear description of such matters as the number and types of occupational specialties, the size of the total population, the jurisdiction of the groups in a society, the existence of differences in wealth, and the staple foods. To maximize the objectivity of these codes, reliance is placed in all cases on the ethnographer's explicit statements. Where these are lacking, the society is given

the classification of "Inadequate Data." Despite such precautions, some errors in classification are certain to appear and scholars may be expected to disagree among themselves concerning still other cases. It is fortunate that, having only 50 societies in our sample, the complete classification can be given here for public inspection and correction. It appears in Appendix I. Interested readers will find that certain other technical problems connected with the method of coding are treated in Appendix III.

A second consideration of general importance for understanding the results of these studies concerns the use of the word "society." In Chapter I it had the loose usage assigned it in common speech. From this point forward it will refer to the relationships among members of the same ultimately sovereign organization. By "ultimately sovereign organization" is meant that group which meets the criteria of sovereignty given below and which is more inclusive in its membership than any other organization acknowledged as sovereign by a particular population.

1. *Sovereign Organizations:* Organizations will be considered sovereign if they exercise original and independent jurisdiction over some sphere of social life. The meaning of these terms is elaborated in Chapter I and Appendix I. At this point, however, we may add certain specific rules for the application of those definitions.

a. The group or its representatives must meet at least once a year.

b. It must have customary procedures for making decisions, such as the declaration of a monarch's will or the taking of a vote or the sounding out of opinions; acknowledged roles, whether formal or informal, which participants hold in decision-making (e.g., representative, officer, voter, audience, nonofficial participant, member, constituent, consultant, king).

c. The group must be considered legitimate by its members. This means that the members must approve of the group's existence, its goals, and its procedure of operation. They may or may not agree with all aspects of the group's organization, but there must not be evidence that they challenge the desirability or justice of its existence or its general purposes and procedures.

d. There must not be evidence which suggests that the group is perceived by its members as failing to persist into the indefinite future.

e. The group must have three or more members.

f. It must make decisions bearing on actions which have a significant effect on its members (e.g., war and peace, the punishment of crimes, the distribution of food, the allocation of the more important means for producing sustenance, the formation of alliances with other groups, the allocation of "civic" duties such as taxes, conscription for military or labor service).

g. It must not be an agency of another organization. This usually eliminates such organizations as armed services, magical and religious organizations, groups of slaves, specialized divisions of a government, specialized divisions of an economy such as the organization which operates a market or which cultivates crops or tends the herds, and educational or socializing organizations such as schools and organized age-sets.

h. It must be viewed as a distinctive organization by the people who are its members and over whom it has jurisdiction.

Further:

i. The nuclear family—that is, any group consisting of the partners to a marriage and the children of their union—will always be called a sovereign organization unless there is clear evidence that its members have little or no attachment to each other. A polygamous family is counted as a single nuclear family.

j. The unit of settlement (e.g., village, town, rural neighborhood) will always be called a sovereign organization unless there is clear evidence that its members have little or no attachment to each other, that its jurisdiction is not original and independent, or that it is in no sense a decision-making group. Units of settlement are defined below.

k. Organizations will be counted as meeting criterion (a) above, if there is an effective obligation among participants to join together for common and customary action under stated circumstances (such as common defense or the sharing of food in time of disaster).

l. When a group seems to meet the foregoing criteria but there is some conflicting evidence, the case will be coded as uncertain.

2. *Nonsovereign Organizations:* These are groups which meet criteria a, b, c, d, e, h, and k for sovereign organizations, but which do not meet one or more of the following criteria for sovereign groups: f, g, or the stipulation that the group's jurisdiction shall be original and independent.

3. *Specialties in Communal Activities:* These are behaviors which conform to the following stipulations:

a. They are performed only by persons who meet some customary criteria of competence.

b. The criteria are not obtained through normal socialization for an age or sex role or a role in the nuclear family.

c. The behaviors concerned are directed primarily toward meeting the needs of some sovereign or nonsovereign organization rather than the needs of particular individuals as such.

Such specialties will almost always include any political offices, magical or religious roles, many educational and socializing roles, and slave labor.

4. *Specialties in Noncommunal Activities:* These are behaviors which meet the criteria presented below:

a. They are not performed by all persons in the society nor by all persons holding a particular age or sex role or a given role in the nuclear family.

b. They are directed primarily toward meeting the needs of one or more individuals, as such, rather than the needs of sovereign or nonsovereign organizations.

c. They involve the production of some object or service (or repair of an object) for the use of some healthy adult member of the unit studied, other than the maker or repairer when the maker or repairer is recognized by the adult served as providing such a special service.[9]

5. *Principal Source of Food:* This is a simple record of the methods used to obtain what the ethnographer reports to be the staple food or foods consumed by members of the society.[10] The categories are:

0. Collecting, gathering
1. Fishing
2. Herding—nomadic
3. Herding—settled
4. Agriculture—root crops
5. Agriculture—grain crops
6. Hunting
7. Hunting or fishing and root crops
8. Hunting or fishing and grain crops
9. Harvesting from trees which require some care if they are to bear a crop.

6. *Amount of Food Produced:* This classification takes into account the quantity of food produced in relation to the needs of the population. It invariably depends on explicit statements by the ethnographer. The categories are:

0. Famine not uncommon.

1. Low—amount a matter of some uncertainty, requiring constant effort to obtain enough to meet minimal requirements.

2. Adequate—there is a general expectation that the amount produced will exceed bare subsistence needs.

3. Plenty—supluses of food are readily obtainable.

7. *Degree of Threat from Armed Attacks by Alien Societies:* Here there are three categories. Further details appear in Appendix I.

0. Little or no likelihood of such attacks or such attacks easily warded off.

1. Some, but not certain, likelihood of such attacks and the success of warding them off is uncertain.

2. Considerable—such attacks are certain to occur and it

is likely that they cannot be warded off successfully; or attacks may occur with uncertain success, but there is also possibility of large casualties, extensive property damage, or subjugation by an invader.

8. *Amount of the Bride Price:* The price, if any, which must be paid to obtain a wife is highly variable among societies. Here it is convenient to make the following classification:

0. None—the ethnographer explicitly reports that no price is charged, or mentions none.

1. Moderate—price exists, but does not involve more than six months of labor on behalf of the bride's family, or does not change the standard of living of the groom's family or its members.

2. Considerable—price charged exceeds the specifications just listed under category 1.

9. *Debts:* This classification records the presence and size of obligations which require individuals or groups to repay loans of goods or services. It does not record such obligations for repayment when the making of the loan and the terms of its repayment are governed by rules of kinship or by such ritual relationships as blood brotherhood. This provision is included to eliminate the less formal and contractual kinds of borrowing which frequently occur and which, presumably, do not reflect the degree of impersonality and specialization of relationship associated with other kinds of debts. The categories are:

0. None—the ethnographer denies that such debt relations exist or fails to mention them.

1. Moderate—some debt relations exist, but there is no

indication that they are frequent or that they are of a size that debtors find difficult to repay.

2. Considerable—debt relations exist and the ethnographer mentions that some debtors find it difficult to repay the loan.

10. *Social Classes:* These are parts of a population which differ in amount of wealth. There need not be any expectation that a family having more wealth than its neighbors will continue in that position for more than one generation. Appendix I should be consulted for further details. Classes are coded as "present" or "absent."

11. *Individually Owned Property:* This refers to property that is important in the production of the society's more significant means of sustenance. Ownership of magical techniques which can be transferred to other people is included if the techniques are thought important in economic productivity. An individual possesses ownership in a property if he alone can legitimately determine some significant aspects of the employment to which it is put, or the allocation of the benefits from its use. Such rights of ownership in a property may be held by more than one person, each individual determining some particular aspect of the property's employment. (Appendix I contains further specifications.) Three categories were devised:

0. Individuals do not own economically significant property.

1. Individuals own property which is used in producing what the ethnographer designates as forms of sustenance, but not those which he calls the most important forms of wealth or the staple foods.

2. Individuals *can* own property employed in producing what the ethnographer designates as the most important forms of wealth or the staple foods.

12. *Unit of Settlement:* Some societies with large populations possess no towns or cities; their people are settled in cattle compounds, in villages, or in nomadic bands in which they wander about with their herds. Others have some or all of the population living in towns. Still others are city-states in which almost all members spend at least part of their lives in a central city. The following conventions were employed to classify units of settlement:

0. Population is settled by households, hamlets, or scattered rural neighborhoods. There are no villages, towns, or cities.

1. Population is settled by villages or encampments, each bringing together at least 50 people, and/or there is a kraal, compound, village, or encampment specially designated as that of a chief or king. There are no towns or cities.

2. Population, or part of it, is settled in one or more towns (a local community of 300 or more people). There are no cities.

3. Population, or part of it, is settled in one or more cities (local communities having 2,000 or more people).

13. *Size of Population:* This refers to the population of the ultimately sovereign organization. In many cases it is estimated by the ethnographer or can be obtained from official census reports. In other cases, it is inferable from other facts. When, for example, we find that the Shoshoni have the nuclear family as their ultimately sovereign unit, we can be quite certain that its population is less than 50.

Again, we can be reasonably certain that the population of Egypt under the Middle Kingdom exceeded 10,000 since we know the size of some of the communities of that period. In other cases, the population may be estimated, though very grossly, from a knowledge of the number of dwelling units inhabited by nuclear families. When instances of this latter type appeared, the number of dwellings was multiplied by five, which was a conservative estimate of the number of persons living in such units given the high death rate among the young.[11] Finally, one can sometimes make a crude estimate of the size of a specific number of ultimately sovereign groups when they are said to have about the same number of members and the entire population of all such groups is provided. The following categories were developed by tabulating these population estimates and trying to distribute them in four equal groups.

- 0. 1–49
- 1. 50–399
- 2. 400–9,999
- 3. 10,000 or more

INTERRELATIONS AMONG INDICATORS

As might be expected, some of these indicators are related to one another. Interested readers may consult Table XXV in Appendix I for a report of these relationships.

SOME PROBLEMS OF INTERPRETATION

There are two rather special problems of interpretation which one must settle in studies such as those that follow.

When may the lack of evidence be taken as evidence, and how shall we speak of the origin of some belief when we lack historical or experimental data concerning its beginnings?

It may seem absurd that no evidence should ever be taken as evidence, but there are situations in which this is not utterly foolish and may be quite necessary. Suppose, for example, that the anthropologist who studies a primitive village reports finding beliefs in water sprites and ancestral spirits, but makes no reference to a deity who created the universe. Shall we assume that such a deity may exist but not be reported by the anthropologist? I propose that, in most cases, we shall not go astray if we conclude that these villagers have no such deity. The reasoning behind such a proposal has two parts. First, all the ethnographers whose work was consulted for this research were reared in Western civilization. The presence of a high, monotheistic god in their own civilization is known to all of them and they are likely to be interested indeed if a similar belief appears among simpler peoples. In fact, the existence of such gods and the nature of the conditions which produce a belief in them have been the subject of a classic professional debate in anthropology. It is unlikely, therefore, that the presence of such a god would fail to be noted. Second, it is quite understandable that observers do not report that which is absent from a society unless its absence is a source of some surprise or special interest. There would be no end to the writing of an ethnographic book if the author had to state everything which he did *not* find! It is hard enough to report all that was observed.

This sort of reasoning will undoubtedly lead us into some errors. It will be pursued, however, because we need judgments about as many of the societies in our sample as possible and because the conditions we seek to classify are such that it is unlikely that Western observers would fail to note their presence.

But what of interpretations concerning the origin of beliefs? Our information almost always states that some belief and a condition which we think might produce it exist side by side in a particular society. It almost never tells us that the belief developed after this condition appeared. It never provides instances in which two societies, identical in all respects except for this crucial condition and belief, can be examined and the presence of the condition in one but not in the other can be related to the presence of the belief in one but not both.

We face a situation common in research. We want to speak of cause and effect, for that is what the term "origin" implies. Yet we have to acknowledge that such language is not justified by the available data. All we will know, in strictest logic, is that a belief and some other condition occur together. We cannot be entirely certain that the condition produced the belief, and it may be that the belief caused the social condition.

After the findings are all before us, we shall return (in Chapter X) to ask whether it is plausible that the religious beliefs produced the social conditions. At this point, however, we can forecast that the evidence we have will support hypotheses about the origin of beliefs, or fail to confirm them, in the following sense: If a given social condition did cause a particular belief, we would expect the two to appear together. If that condition did not produce a particular belief, one would be as likely as not to occur without the other. Therefore, the appearance of condition and belief together more frequently than chance alone would allow is consistent with, though not proof of, the conclusion that one of these caused the other.

A NOTE ON LEVELS OF SIGNIFICANCE AND TABULATION

Unless stated otherwise, all hypotheses given in succeeding chapters were formulated before the data with which they are tested were examined. In such cases, levels of significance are reported for one tail of the probability distribution. Relationships are termed significant if they reach the .05 level of probability.[12]

Further, unless stated otherwise, all levels of significance were obtained from a computation of chi-square values. These computations were corrected for continuity in all four-celled tables in which the expected value in a cell was less than ten. Chi-square values computed for tables of more than four cells were automatically corrected for continuity by the method employed, namely, that of maximum likelihood ratios.[13]

Finally, we may note the way in which the 50 societies were divided in setting up some of the tables that appear in later chapters. Whenever we arrange societies by some continuous criterion, say the size of their populations, we must decide how they should be grouped in the tables. Unless there is a statement to the contrary, these groupings were always made on some such arbitrary basis as dividing our cases as nearly as possible into halves or thirds or quarters.

CONCLUSION

These pages have described the sample of societies from which our information is drawn and certain indices which are employed frequently in the chapters which follow. We may now turn to those chapters for the findings from our study, beginning with an explanation of monotheistic beliefs in the simpler societies.

CHAPTER III

MONOTHEISM

Paul Radin once said:

. . . To the average man [monotheism] signifies the belief in an uncreated, Supreme Deity, wholly beneficent, omnipotent, omniscient and omnipresent: it demands the complete exclusion of all other gods. The world in its most minute details is regarded as His work, as having been created out of nothing in response to His wish. . . . and any assumption that He can act through the intermediation of other deities is idolatry by implication, even though He has expressly given these deities their forms, their attributes and their powers. . . .[1]

Such a god is rarely found. Even in the highly developed monotheism of Judaism and Christianity, God shares the supernatural world with demons, angels, Satan, and such honored dead as the saints. True, He created this cloud of beings, but they have an existence of their own and exhibit distinctive purposes. In similar fashion, the Mohammedan god, Allah, is surrounded by other supernatural beings.

Judaism, Christianity, and Mohammedanism are monotheistic beliefs, not in the sense that God is the only supernatural being nor in the sense that God forces all other supernatural beings into a monolithic uniformity of desire and function. Instead, they are monotheistic religions in specifying God as the first cause of all effects and the necessary and sufficient condition for reality's continued existence.

A few primitive and ancient peoples have a similar conception of God. In addition, many of the simpler societies believe in a deity who is the sole creator of the universe. There also are some peoples who know of a god who rules the world and heavens, even though it is not clear that he created them. We shall call such deities as these "high gods" to signify that they are considered ultimately responsible for all events, whether as history's creator, its director, or both. In this sense of providing a single deity as the ultimate source of events in nature and supernature, these religious beliefs are monotheistic, as are the great religions which first appeared in Asia Minor.

THE NATURE OF HIGH GODS

Some of these high gods among the simpler peoples are known for the single act of producing reality. After that creation they took no further interest in the natural or supernatural orders. Men may commemorate them, but worship and sacrifice are not directed toward these distant, disinterested beings. Other supernaturals, brought into being by the high god, control the rain and winds and harvest, and guide the hunter to his prey and the fisherman to his catch. These later deities become the objects of human hope and fear, the determinants of events important to men.

Still other high gods, having spawned the universe, restrict their interest in it to one or a few of its aspects. They may keep order among other deities. They may find special interest in the performance of some human ceremony such as the initiation of the young or the celebration of the new year. They may intervene to help isolated or desolate creatures while giving little attention to those whose lives are pursued successfully in the company of their kind. The list of such special interests is, of course, very long.

There are also, as we have noted, high gods who rule the universe they did not produce. It is typical in such cases that the beginning of both the natural and supernatural orders is not explained at all or is attributed to some unknown cause. Once these orders have begun, however, the high god exercises control over their course, whether in person or through deputies.

Finally, we discover that those high gods who take an active part in earthly affairs may or may not be concerned with human morality. Some are. Others govern the crops or warfare or the seasons, but seem not to care whether virtue triumphs or the wicked go unpunished.

In short, every high god is, in some sense, the determiner of all events which occur. The means by which he does this and the motives and attitudes which he brings to the task vary from one society to another. Our first problem is to explain how the conception of a high god could arise.

THE ORIGIN OF HIGH GODS

A possible explanation is the one usually advanced by the primitives themselves. They speak of having direct or indirect contacts with the god. Perhaps he appears to them in visions or riding among the clouds. Perhaps his presence is inferred from the death of an evil man or from a successful cattle raid which followed sacrifices to the deity. Ideas of this kind do not lend themselves to satisfactory empirical tests, and we shall not pursue them further.

By contrast, we may examine three explanations which

might be subjected to increasingly precise efforts at verification as empirical knowledge develops. The first sees monotheism as the original human theology which was painfully regained in some places only after an interlude of other beliefs. The second states that the notion of a high god appears at all times and places, but is accepted at only a few. The third links monotheistic ideas to a particular organization of human social life.

The first of these three accounts is that of an Austrian Jesuit who was also an anthropologist, Father Wilhelm Schmidt.[2] Father Schmidt's essential argument assumes that the simplest peoples are also, organizationally, the oldest, and that all of them worship high gods. He declared that such a high god is almost always characterized by his devotees as eternal, omniscient, beneficent, omnipotent, the creator of reality, and the founder and support of human morality. As some societies became more complex and specialized, developing either patrilineal or matrilineal cultures, the original and ubiquitous monotheism was distorted into animisms, polytheisms, or cults of the dead. In Schmidt's thinking, this rationale is convincing because it is consonant with the facts of human history and the nature of man. Man, he proposes, requires the concept of a Supreme Being. Such a concept satisfies all human needs. It provides a rational cause for reality, it explains social needs and guides their expression by showing how men should relate to one another, it supports moral needs, and it satisfies the emotional desires for trust, love, and thankfulness.

. . . Thus in all these attributes this exalted figure furnished primitive man with the ability and the power to live and to love, to trust and to work, the prospect of becoming the master of the world and not its slave, and the aspiration to attain to yet higher, super-mundane goals.[3]

Apart from the research of Father Schmidt and his disciples, there is no support for Schmidt's judgment that those societies which have the simplest forms of organization are also worshippers of high gods. We shall, in fact, find many examples to the contrary.

The absence of independent corroboration has not changed the position of most of Schmidt's followers, and for an excellent reason: they can usually raise the possibility that the anthropologist responsible for the counterinstance did not adequately investigate religion in the society he studied, hence did not find the high god. Or, it may be averred that evidence for belief in a high god was present all along in the dissenter's data, but he failed to see the correct interpretation. Or, in some cases, it can be argued that the society studied in the counterinstance is not really simple in organization, or that its simplicity, hence its theology, has been subtly corrupted by contacts with neighboring peoples.

Almost all non-Schmidtian anthropologists remain unconvinced by the Austrian's position. It is clear that this dispute cannot be resolved until both parties can agree on a precise statement of the kind of evidence which could support or cast doubt on Schmidt's theory. For our purposes, we shall assume, with most professional anthropologists, that existing evidence does not support Father Schmidt.

The conception of monotheism as the universally present theology is also found in Paul Radin's essay on *Monotheism Among Primitive Peoples*.[4] Long interested in the anthropology of religion, Radin concludes that monotheistic beliefs are the expression of a kind of temperament—a temperament which is found among some individuals in all cultures. These men—poets, philosophers, priests—give utterance to definitely monotheistic beliefs. They always picture the world as a unified whole, always postulate some First Cause. Radin suggests, however, that this conception is not widely held in any society and proposes that, since most people are practical and realistic, existing creeds represent some compromise between the masses and the idealistic monotheists. This leaves the question of presenting the conditions under which monotheism becomes the prevailing and exclusive official religion of a particular society. Radin states that these conditions will be "facts of a general sociological order." [5] Unfortunately, he does not elaborate on this statement.

As with Schmidt's theory of man's Fall from original monotheism, there is no adequate empirical support for Radin's idea of the universality of monotheistic conceptions among primitive savants or among persons having a particular quality of mind. Radin himself made no wide-ranging test of his scheme and existing studies of primitives are unlikely to afford him the kind of facts he would require. Further, even if we accepted Radin's judgment, we should still have to locate those facts "of a general sociological order" which explain why only some societies have high gods.

One suggestion of what those facts might be is found in the work of the archaelogist, James Breasted.[6] From his study of the Egyptian high god Aton whose worship was developed under Pharaoh Ikhnaton, Breasted proposes that monotheistic beliefs may be stimulated by experience with powerful human rulers who govern great and complex kingdoms and empires. This suggestion cannot be dismissed out of hand. It may have some validity in cases like that of ancient Egypt. However, we can be certain that it is not a generally applicable account of monotheism's origins when we find, as we shall, beliefs in omnipresent and all powerful high gods in societies which lack any suggestion of strong, centralized, human leadership.

The proposals of Schmidt, Radin, and Breasted do not exhaust those available, but they suggest the range of answers given to the problem of monotheism's origins and they represent perhaps the most conspicuous current solutions. Each has deficiencies as a testable and universally applicable explanation of beliefs in high gods. Each may account, in part, for the presence of monotheism in particular places and times. We shall return to these proposals after presenting a fourth, and shall see what this newer theory suggests about its predecessors.

If we follow out the ideas with which this book began, we should expect the notion of a high god to correspond in some manner to the purposive decision-making processes of particular societies. What might those processes be? For clues, we may refer again to the essentials of a monotheistic belief.

Monotheisms, we have found, assume that all the events which men know have a common source. They assume that this source is a being, a supernatural being. Through the action of this being, diverse events are unified.

From the introductory chapter, we may repeat certain further premises. The first is that every deity corresponds in some sense to the constitutional structure of a sovereign group. The second states that the events which deities influence are those of concern to the sovereign groups to which these deities correspond.

Such premises might suggest that we shall find a high god whenever a sovereign group is concerned with creating diverse events or bringing order among them. However, it is obvious that such an explanation of monotheism is inadequate since all human groups have these interests. On the other hand, to propose that we should seek instances in which there exist groups organized to control all of nature—humanity, the movements of heavenly bodies and of subatomic particles, and all the rest—would be equally futile, since no such groups are known to exist.

Fortunately, there are ways of escaping from these alternatives. If we search for the conditions which correspond to the idea of a high god, and if we assume that these conditions will involve the actions of sovereign groups, then we seek situations in which such groups bring unity to the world's diversity. Sovereign groups do this to at least a part of the world when they review, judge, or modify the actions of subordinate groups or individuals. All peoples have some sovereign group that influences the individuals who are its members. Monotheism, however, does not appear everywhere. Therefore we shall focus our attention on those cases in which sovereign organizations have other groups subordinate to them.

But we can go further toward specifying a solution to the origin of monotheism. Belief in a high god is a belief that all experienced events are ordered by his action. The key word for our next step is "experienced." Let us assume that the individual experiences the environment as ordered to the extent that it conforms to legitimate, normative, social rules. The widest area over which such rules prevail is that governed by the ultimate, legitimate, decision-making and rule-enforcing group to which he gives allegiance. For some primitive peoples this group may be the village. For modern industrial societies, this group is the nation-state. Beyond its boundaries there is no dependable rule of its laws.

We can also say that a being who brings order among others subordinate to him must have available a minimum of two such others if he is to perform his activity. He must have at least two such subordinates at hand in order to create a relationship between them. This should mean that a conception of a high god will require the presence of at least three types of groups arranged in a hierarchy.

The phrase "types of" groups appears as a crucial part of the expectation we shall test. Suppose, for example, we find a series of sovereign groups in which a kingdom contains villages and the villages consist of nuclear families. We shall count this as a situation in which three different *types* of sovereign groups appear and shall not be concerned with the number of villages or the even larger number of families. The rationale for counting the *types of sovereign groups rather than the number of such groups* is taken from studies of large organizations. The procedures of higher management are devised for classes of employees and varieties of subordinate organizations, not for individual workers or for each particular subsidiary division of the firm. If this were not the case, the relationship of upper management to every subordinate individual would be a unique case demanding special attention. It would then become quite impossible for managers to pay attention to major problems confronting their organizations. They would be lost in a morass of details. Further, special treatment for each employee and each subsidiary division of the concern would encourage a kind of competition for favors among employees and divisions which could work only to the destruction of the organization's ability to operate smoothly, to achieve a set of organizational goals. We shall assume that societies are not different in these respects from other organizations—hence we shall count the types of sovereign groups rather than the number of such groups. It is only for the sake of sparing readers needless repetition that the phrase "types of" will not appear throughout this chapter. It is implied at all points in the expectations about monotheism.

Finally, we may judge that the subordinate groups in the series must, like the one which is superordinate, be sovereign. This should be true because our high god is to provide unity in diversity, and the subordinate purposes which he organizes must be sufficiently different from his own to make clear that he does indeed modify them and bring them together. Subordinate groups which are but departments of the superordinate or expressions of some aspect of its purposes can scarcely fulfill this function. It is likely that their central purposes will be those of the superordinate body itself. We need not review the details of this argument from Chapter I. Its importance lies in its applicability to our present problem.

FINDINGS

To summarize, we shall expect to find evidence of monotheism where, counting out from the individual to the boundary of his society, there are three or more types of sovereign groups ranked in hierarchical order. The methods for identifying sovereign groups were described in Chapter II. They may now be applied to our 50 societies. Table I gives the result.

TABLE I

NUMBER OF SOVEREIGN GROUPS AND PRESENCE OF HIGH GOD

Presence of High God	Number of Sovereign Groups		
	One or two	Three	Four or more
Present	2	7	10
Absent	17	2	1
Total	19	9	11
Per cent present	11	78	91

There are 39 cases in which the presence or absence of a high god could be determined with reasonable certainty. Unless the high god is very active in human affairs, anthropologists tend to present only the briefest description of his nature and functions. In this, however, they perhaps follow the lead of their informants. People do not take much interest in an otiose—that is, an indolent—deity nor are they likely to clarify their views of him. As a consequence, the native informant, like the observer, may have only a vague, confused, and sparse idea about an inactive high god. For this study, the significance of such a result requires particular care in seeking for monotheistic deities who may be given but passing mention in published reports.

Of the 19 societies having fewer than three sovereign groups, 17 lack monotheism. Of the 20 societies having three or more such groups, 17 possess a high god. The probability of so great a difference occurring by chance is less than .0005.[7]

The coefficient of contingency is .57 which, when corrected for the number of cells in the table, becomes about .81.[8]

This result supports the prediction from which it springs. To evaluate it further, let us consider three additional points: 1) the problems which, for 11 societies, made it impossible to judge with certainty whether a high god was present, 2) the five cases in Table I which do not conform to our expectations, and 3) the possibility that certain other explanations will account as well as our own for the findings just reported.

THE IDENTITY OF THE HIGH GODS

Even a brief description of the qualities of the high gods tabulated above may help to make concrete and understandable the rather abstract discussion up to this point. These descriptions are given for the 19 societies in which clear evidence of such a deity was available. Then descriptions appear for the 11 societies about which no firm decision concerning monotheism could be made.

1. Azande—Worship an omnipotent supreme being who created reality. There is no systematic thought about his relations to other spirits. The Azande pray to him when ill or in trouble and perform ceremonies of thanksgiving to him. This god gave men their culture, including knowledge of magic. He has no influence on human morality.

2. Aztec—Believed in a god who created reality and who was ineffable.

3. Bemba—Refer to a high god who is the original source of the magic through which daily affairs are conducted. He sends children to men and controls the thunder.

4. Carib—Speak of a vague supreme deity who is in charge of the universe. He is reality's first cause. He is beneficent but capable of anger, vaguely known and rarely discussed.

5. Carrier—There is a supreme being in the sky. He helps unfortunate people. Beliefs about him are vague.

6. Cuna—Believe in a god who created reality, and who sternly enforces conventional morality, punishing immodesty, loose talk, theft, and adultery.

7. Egyptians—In one form or another, the ancient Egyptians conceived of a high god both before and after the famous monotheistic period under Pharaoh Ikhnaton. This deity, by whatever name, was active in human affairs, concerned with the morality of men, and, in the era of the Egyptian empire, conceived of as Lord of the Universe.[9]

8. Ganda—Katonda was the father of the gods. He and his offspring created all else.

9. Ifaluk—The major gods had a forefather. His descendants created reality.

10. Iroquois—The major gods had a grandmother. Together, they created reality. The grandmother is the divinity of death and rules the land of the dead.

11. Israelites—Yahweh created all reality which he now governs actively. He supports human moral codes.

12. Lengua—A beetle created all things. He takes no interest in his creation.

13. Lozi—The high god created all reality. The Lozi pray to him for good crops. Rituals concerning hunting, burial, and bad dreams are focused on him. Lozi royalty are descended directly from him.

14. Miao—The greatest of all gods lives in the sky and controls heaven and earth. Sometimes he sends his daughter to succor poor and unfortunate men.

15. Nuer—There is a god who created all things and now governs them. He punishes all immorality and rewards virtue. He does not punish humans who err accidentally. The dead go to join him. The Nuer pray to him, regard him as ineffable and benevolent.

16. Nyakyusa—Above all other deities is a supreme being who is omnipresent. He is not very active in earthly affairs, but he does send devils to punish men who do not feed and respect their ancestors, removing these tormentors only when their victims sincerely repent.

17. Tanala—There is a supreme being who gives life and who defends the poor and helpless. Destiny or fate, which determines all things, is his will. It operates mechanistically. This god is rarely invoked.

18. Yahgan—There is a god who is master and ruler of reality. He lives in the heavens, is good and benevolent. He owns the animals and plants. He gives and takes life. Many prayers are offered to him.

19. Zulu—Unkulunkulu created everything. He died long ago and so is not worshipped. The accounts of him are vague and conflicting.

The following are the 11 ambiguous cases.

1. Aymara—It appears that these people adopted the Inca belief in Viracocha who, rising from Lake Titicaca, created everything. There is great unclarity, however, whether this is a serious belief or whether they are just repeating an old and familiar Inca legend.

2. Blackfoot—The accounts vary greatly in describing

the Sun as a true high god or as one of a polytheistic pan-
theon.

3. Karen—These people have two sets of creation stories
and the sources do not clarify the relations between them.
In one, a god named Y'wa is the creator of all things. He
is described as eternal, everlasting, omnipotent, and the sup-
porter of morality. At the same time, he is not worshipped.
The Karen are described as believing that he leaves them to
their fate. The second tale makes no mention of Y'wa, attributes creation to Edolius (a kind of bird) and Termite.
The best evidence is that both stories had indigenous origins.

4. Lepcha—The accounts describe a Creative Mother
who, together with her husband, lives under the world. Her
children are representatives of the various aspects of reality.
Since, among the Lepcha the father is never important in
mythology, it is possible that this Creative Mother may be
considered the source of reality. The accounts are not clear
on this point.

5. Nandi—The best report about these people makes
what seem to be conflicting statements about their belief
in the Sun. On the one hand, there is a specific denial that
the Nandi know a high god; on the other, there are statements that the Sun personifies the powers of nature and the
universe and that all other supernaturals stand intermediate
between the Sun and man.

6. Pomo—The published accounts report that Coyote or
Marumda created man, but whether they were thought to
create any or all other things is unclear.

7. Romans—Although one might expect that evidence
here would be entirely adequate, it is not. The most author-
itative accounts present arguments supporting and denying

the idea that Jupiter was conceived as a high god. At the time of interest for our sample, the Augustan period, the monotheism of the Stoics and the mystery religions was known in Rome, but the extent of its penetration at this time is in doubt.

8. Tallensi—The Earth is alive and all men are subject to its rule. Earth is the source of prosperity, fertility, and health, and is concerned with the good of all Tallensi. Whether Earth created or rules the heavens is ambiguous.

9. Tiv—The Heavens are said to be responsible for creation. It is not clear whether this refers to one or more supernatural beings.

10. Winnebago—A mighty spirit, Earthmaker, is said to have created everything, but, at other points, seems to have made only the earth and its contents.

11. Yurok—There are tales of a vague deity who liberated fish for men's use and let babies come out of women instead of allowing them to stay in the womb and kill the mother. These stories sometimes suggest that this god is taken as a kind of supreme being, but no definite statement can be made on the matter.

It may be of interest that seven of these 11 societies have a hierarchy of three or more sovereign groups, four do not. Thus, even if we added them as instances of monotheism, the relationship expressed in Table I would not be changed appreciably.

THE NEGATIVE EVIDENCE

Five of the 39 societies tabulated do not fit our expectations. Such cases are particularly valuable because they often provide problems for further study. Let us examine them one by one, beginning with those in which societies having fewer than three sovereign groups are reported to believe in high gods. They are the Lengua and the Yahgan.

The sovereign groups in Lengua society are the household and the clan-village. There is no instrument of native government beyond the village although villages have joined together to fight inroads on their land by the Paraguayan government. The creation myth is clearly monotheistic as the term is defined in this study. We must count this as an instance which definitely violates our prediction. Unfortunately, the data do not suggest why the Lengua should deviate from our expectation.

The Yahgan of Tierra del Fuego are a very simple people whose sovereign units include the individual and the household. Beyond these there are loosely defined neighborhoods of families scattered along the shoreline. The typical neighborhood is also a patrilocal kinship group. The accounts do not suggest that these neighborhoods have any political organization, although their inhabitants do conduct joint ceremonies of initiation for the young and collaborate to repulse raids by others on their collecting and fishing preserves. It is possible that these neighborhoods are better organized than the reports picture them. Another consideration, however, is the powerful and active figure of the Yahgan high god. He is no distant indifferent spirit, but a dominant ruler. While we cannot eliminate the possibility that the Yahgan provide a case for which our prediction does not hold, it is worth noting that our information about them comes primarily from Martin Gusinde, a follower of Father Schmidt, whose theory would lead one to expect monotheism among this simple, isolated people. As in any research, one would have more confidence in Gusinde's report if it were given independent and impartial corroboration.

Now we may turn to the three remaining deviant cases, those in which societies possessing at least three sovereign groups do not have a monotheistic deity. They are the Orokaiva, Timbira, and Yokuts.

The sovereign groups of Orokaiva society are the household, clan, and village. Perhaps our error is not real, but a matter of falsely separating the clan from the village. Closer inspection of the monograph describing these people reveals that clan and village are often, but not always, one. The author tells us that clans are ceremonial and fighting units, that they own the garden land of which each family operates a section. The clan elders make decisions for other members of the group and the oldest competent man among them acts as chief. We also find that all nonclan members are potential enemies. At the same time, there are many suggestions in the account that villages may consist of members of more than one clan and have their own government. It is, therefore, ambiguous whether this case is a genuine deviant from our expectation or merely an error in coding.

The Timbira are described in great detail and with unusual appreciation for their inner life by an anthropologist, Nimuendaju, who was adopted into their ranks. His depiction tells of four groups which seem to meet our criteria for a sovereign unit, the household, extended family, village, and tribe. The most embracive deities are the Sun and Moon who prove to be unrelated to one another. They create men by diving into a brook. There is no indication that either produced reality or that one created the other. The Sun is somewhat the more potent of the two. This evidence suggests that the Timbira do not meet our expectation.

The final exception to our prediction is that of the Yokuts. These Indians of California's San Joaquin valley appear to have had three sovereign groups, the household, village, and tribe. Each village was organized under a headman. The tribes are described as politically independent of one another because each had a chief who received support from the villages under his jurisdiction and who had the services of a herald to communicate with his people. The whole tribe acted as a unit in time of war. On the other hand, there is evidence that the principal functions of the chief may have been ceremonial rather than the exercise or co-ordination of tribal sovereignty. Further, village autonomy was such that the headmen of all villages had to agree before any tribal action could be undertaken. These facts raise the possibility that the Yokuts were misclassified as having three sovereign groups and therefore are not an exception to our prediction.

In summary, there are two societies which seem not to conform to the prediction that, where three or more sovereign groups appear, a high god will also be found and that such a god will not be present in societies with fewer than three such groups. These societies are the Lengua and Timbira. Two other negative cases may be due to misclassification. These are the Orokaiva and Yokuts. A final society, that of the Yahgan, is difficult to appraise in relation to our prediction because many professional anthropologists doubt the validity of the available descriptions concerning the presence of a high god.

ALTERNATIVE EXPLANATIONS

While one cannot foresee all possible alternative explanations for any finding, there are some additional factors which might plausibly account for our results and which require further exploration. Unfortunately, the size of our sample makes it impossible to do much by way of holding several things constant while varying the number of sovereign groups. This limits the pursuit of certain alternative accounts.

First of all, let us see if, in enumerating the number of sovereign groups in our societies, we have evolved only one of many measures of social complexity, any one of which would predict monotheism as well as our measure. A collection of such potential measures is described in Chapter II. They are: the presence of debt relations, the number of communal specialties, the number of noncommunal specialties, the number of nonsovereign groups, the presence of differences in wealth, the existence of individual holdings of economically significant property, the size of the unit of settlement, and the size of the population in the society's ultimately sovereign group. Only two of these eight indices of complexity fail to be independent of monotheism when the .50 level of confidence is used as a criterion. One exception, the number of noncommunal specialties, is positively related to monotheism at the .10 level. The second exception, the number of nonsovereign groups, is positively related to monotheism at the .01 level of probability.

We may ask whether, by holding the number of noncommunal specialties constant, we eliminate the relation of the number of sovereign groups to the presence of high gods. The answer is negative. The relationship holds among societies having no specialized roles of this type and among societies having one or more of such roles. The respective significance levels [10] are .02 and .01. Similar results appear when the other indicators of complexity are held constant. Finally, the relation between monotheism and the number of non-sovereign groups vanishes when the number of sovereign groups is held constant.

These findings indicate that several plausible indicators of social complexity other than the number of sovereign groups are not directly and significantly related to the presence of high gods. In addition, the data show that, when number of sovereign groups is held constant, the relations between monotheism and either number of noncommunal specialties or nonsovereign groups become quite insignificant. We cannot, of course, rule out the possibility that complex interactions exist between these eight indicators of complexity and monotheism. The number of cases in the sample does not permit us to explore this possibility.

The findings from these 50 societies do, in addition, run counter to what one might expect from Father Schmidt's theory. The societies with the fewest sovereign groups are least likely to possess high gods. Eight other indices of organizational complexity are not significantly related to monotheism.

The data also have some bearing on Breasted's suggestion that monotheism appears when people have before them the model of a powerful, centralized government. While such a model may be a sufficient condition for monotheism, it is not necessary. Less than half of the monotheistic peoples in our sample are organized into kingdoms, and not all of the kingdoms are strongly centralized. It is true that, since kingdoms tend to have more sovereign units subordinated to them than do other systems of more than two sovereign groups, the development of monotheism in kingdoms tends, correspondingly, to be more elaborate. By contrast, however, the three cases in our sample which have the most extensively developed conception of a high god and which make that deity most important in human affairs are not kingdoms. In fact, none of these three had strong, centralized governments. They are the Israelites in the time of the Judges, and the modern Nuer and Cuna. In each case, decisions are made by councils of adults or elders. In each case, such leaders as there are tend to have powers which come from expressing the community's consensus or customs, not those required to promote or enforce strong, independent policies of their own.

But Breasted's suggestion leads us to another important possibility concerning our findings. If we generalized his idea, we might ask whether, though not produced by the presence of a king, monotheism might tend to appear when some other specific type of sovereign unit occurs as third in a series of three or more. Or, we could inquire whether a particular type of ultimately sovereign unit is connected with monotheism. Although our data provide a negative answer to both these questions, the reliability of the detailed code of types of units is not sufficient to allow much confidence in these results (see Appendix III). For the record, however, the classification shows that, among the third units in societies which have monotheism are one neighborhood, three villages, two districts, one town and seven chiefdoms. Those seven societies in which the third unit is exclusively or additionally a kinship group contain, as third units, one case each of an extended family and a gens, two clans, a phratry, and two tribes. Similarly scattered results appear when we consider the distribution of our monotheistic societies by the type of ultimately sovereign units which they possess. More conclusive answers to these questions must await a more reliable code.

While we are discussing alternatives to our explanation of the belief in high gods, we might consider again the wish-fulfillment theories of religion mentioned in Chapter I. One extrapolation from such accounts might assert, with Father Schmidt, that the most satisfying belief for a people to have would be the conception of a loving, powerful, nurturing high god, whose gracious rule would keep the universe in order. One might also expect that such a belief would be most likely to appear where people needed it most, that is where conditions of life were most threatening.

The data of our study provide no support for such an extrapolation. We find, to the contrary, that monotheism, and especially elaborate monotheistic beliefs, are most likely to appear in societies which have the most stable sources of food, namely a settled agriculture which produces grains. The probability level associated with this relationship is beyond the .02 level. Such relationship as we can make to the plentifulness of the food supply also shows a positive relationship to monotheism, although the probability level reaches only .10.

The finding of a relationship between the raising of grain as the staple food and the presence of monotheism is not surprising. As many previous studies have shown, complexity of social organization requires increased resources to permit its appearance and sustain its functioning.[11] As one kind of complex development, an increase in the number of sovereign groups is likely to be associated with such an enrichment of resources.

HIGH GODS AND HUMAN AFFAIRS

As we have seen, some high gods play no active role in human affairs. After they created the universe, they became otiose, that is without any part or function in current human affairs. Other high gods do take an active part in the lives of men, and of these, some reward or punish people in accordance with the way men treat their fellows.

If the concept of a high god corresponds to experience with unifying purpose, one might presume that, as the workings of that purpose became stronger and more evident, the high god would be seen as more active. In terms of our indices, we should expect that the greater the number of sovereign groups in excess of two, the more likely the high god will be active and even concerned with human morality.

Table II shows that the data exhibit a slight tendency in the expected direction. The relationship is not significant, however, providing a level of probability beyond only .70.

Our coded data allow us to test a second explanation of otiosity. Some societies possess many nonsovereign groups that provide communal services—education, medical care, military protection, and the like. Others do not. Such groups make decisions. They are not sovereign, however, because they lack an area of independent and original jurisdiction. They are communal because they get their jurisdiction and goals by delegation from sovereign organizations. They carry out some particular objectives of sovereign groups.

TABLE II

NUMBER OF SOVEREIGN GROUPS AND NATURE OF HIGH GOD

Nature of High God	Number of Sovereign Groups		
	One or two	Three	Four or more
Active: moral	1	1	4
Active	0	1	2
Otiose	1	5	3
Total	2	7	10
Per cent active: moral	50	14	40
Per cent active	0	14	20

One might predict, therefore, that the several purposes of a sovereign group will more likely be seen as active in human affairs if each is embodied in a specific organization. Extending this argument, one might expect that high gods would be conceived as active in human affairs when the complex of purposes they represent is given "hands and feet" by embodiment in nonsovereign communal groups. Table III shows the findings relevant to this theory. Our data provide

TABLE III

NUMBER OF NONSOVEREIGN COMMUNAL GROUPS AND NATURE OF HIGH GOD IN SOCIETIES HAVING AT LEAST THREE SOVEREIGN GROUPS

Nature of High God	Number of Nonsovereign Communal Groups	
	None or One	Two or More
Active: moral	0 *	5 #
Active	0 *	3 #
Otiose	7	2
Total	7	10
Per cent active	0	80

*, #—Combined for Fisher exact test.

significant support for this explanation. (The probability from Fisher's exact test is less than .005.)

We should, however, refine our analysis. Other things equal, the societies that have larger numbers of sovereign groups also tend to have more nonsovereign, communal groups. Table IV repeats the analysis just provided in Table III, but holds number of sovereign groups constant by dividing the number of nonsovereign, communal groups in each society by the number of sovereign organizations. Once again we find a significant relationship between the activity of high gods and the number of nonsovereign, communal groups. The significance level is beyond .05 by Fisher's exact test.

TABLE IV

NUMBER OF NONSOVEREIGN, COMMUNAL GROUPS CORRECTED FOR NUMBER OF SOVEREIGN GROUPS AND NATURE OF HIGH GODS IN SOCIETIES HAVING AT LEAST THREE SOVEREIGN GROUPS

Nature of High God	Ratio of Nonsovereign, Communal Groups to Number of Sovereign Groups	
	.00–.50	.51 or greater
Active: moral	1 *	4 #
Active	1 *	2 #
Otiose	7	2
Total	9	8
Per cent active	22	75

*, #—Combined for Fisher exact test.

These findings suggest another possibility. Perhaps the number of nonsovereign communal groups in a society really measures the degree of occupational specialization. It might be that high gods are active where occupational specialties abound.

This notion is not supported by our data. Among the societies with high gods, neither the number of communal specialties nor noncommunal specialties is related to the otiosity of these deities. It seems that specific purposes must be embodied in *organized groups, not* merely in *social roles*, if high gods are to be active.

We shall be able to continue this discussion of otiosity in Chapter IX. That chapter contains additional theoretical ideas which permit a new approach to the problem.

SUMMARY OF RESULTS

1. Monotheism is positively related to the presence of a hierarchy of three or more sovereign groups in a society.[12]

2. There is no relationship between the number of sovereign groups in such a hierarchy, and the likelihood that the monotheistic deity will be seen as active in earthly affairs including the support of human moral relationships. High gods do tend to be active in societies having two or more non-sovereign communal groups.

3. A variety of other indices of social complexity are not related to the presence of monotheistic beliefs in a society.

4. The data seem to run counter to the expectation of certain anthropologists that a highly developed monotheism would be likely to appear in the simplest and most isolated societies.

CHAPTER IV

POLYTHEISM

For generations, children in Europe and America have learned the names and characters of the deities of ancient times. They discover that Poseidon ruled the seas of classic Greece while Demeter governed agriculture and Hermes' winged feet sped the messages of the gods. They learn how Mars helped the Romans in battle and Minerva provided wisdom in the industries of peace as in the arts of war, while, further to the north, the Germanic Frigga presided over the sky, marriage, and the home, and Thor sent thunder roaring through the heavens.

None of these are high gods as we understood that term in the last chapter, but all of them are great. Each controls all men who engage in any phase of those activities associated with the god. These spirits are the subject of this chapter. They may very well exist together with the notion of a high god in the catalogue of a society's beliefs. We shall search for the conditions which might evoke a belief in their existence. We shall call them "superior gods."

THE NATURE OF THE SUPERIOR GODS

It is often easier to grasp the nature of something if we can contrast it with something else. To that end, we may compare the superior gods with other spirits common among primitive societies. Some spirits are associated with a single, limited population or place. Thus the Aymara of Peru and Bolivia believe that a different deity dwells in each mountain and in many prominent rocks. The Iban of Sarawak feel that the rice planted by each family has its own governing spirits. The Orokaiva of New Guinea associate a special godling with each house in their villages. Among many American Indian tribes, most adults have a unique guardian spirit who takes a part in their personal affairs.

By contrast, the superior gods are not so narrowly limited. Poseidon, as god of the sea, governed the activities of all men when they depended on the waters. He controlled conditions affecting commercial shipping, naval engagements, fishing, and bathing. Demeter ruled the stages in the agricultural cycle in all places. Further, unlike the Iban's rice gods, Demeter governed the raising of agricultural produce by all men. Diana, Roman goddess of the wood and helper of women in childbirth, likewise influenced the experiences of all men in their activities in all forests. All wild plants and animals also fell under her jurisdiction. Thor governed all warfare, and gave strength to every man in activities requiring it.

We may say, then, that the superior gods are more abstract conceptions than the spirits who control particular people or places. Superior gods affect the lives of all men engaged in activities relevant to the gods' interests in all times and places.

At this point we come to a peculiarity in the ethnographic reports which makes for some difficulty in our work. It is not uncommon for an observer to tell us that some named deity, say the Sun or Moon or Morning Star or Bear or

Coyote, is important in a particular society. Unfortunately, many ethnographers do not expand on this point. They do not say just what functions these important deities perform. We are therefore unable to say whether or not these are among the superior gods. In the tabulations made for this chapter, such ambiguous cases are reported separately.[1]

THE ORIGIN OF SUPERIOR GODS

What human experiences might these superior gods represent? Their specialized but abstract natures provide a clue.

Let us suppose that superior gods represent the presence of specialized purposes in human affairs.[2] One might then conclude that the more clearly defined such purposes become —the more sharply distinguishable they are from one another—the more likely they will be conceived as embodied in a superior god. We shall expect, therefore, that such gods will appear when certain human activities become so clearly differentiated from other concerns that particular individuals have them as their principal responsibility. Thus, in some societies, all men fish and hunt and plant and engage in war. In other societies, certain men are primarily responsible for fishing, others have special responsibilities for the conduct of hunting, and still others are specialists in other activities. Each adult in the societies with fewer specialists may perform a great many activities. However, when different activities become clearly distinguished as the occupations of some, but not all, adults, a model for the superior gods is present.

There are, however, not one but two types of specialization classified among our indicators. One has to do with types of specialization in communal activities, the other with types of specialization in noncommunal activities. The former raises a special problem in prediction.

When some men specialize in certain communal activities—as chiefs or governmental accountants or military officers, for example—they have different occupations from their fellows, and their activities are correspondingly distinguished from those of others. At the same time, communal activities, however specialized, are such that they bind people together in a common organization and make possible the functioning of that common organization. They are, as we saw before, agents and instrumentalities of other centers of purpose. In themselves, they do not have original and independent jurisdiction; they do not make the policies they execute. These several considerations make prediction difficult. Shall we say that the agents of communal activities are specialists, thus implying that they are models for a conception of superior gods? Or, shall we emphasize the fact that the purposes these specialists represent are not their own, but are shared by all loyal members of the sovereign groups whose bidding they do? Shall we conclude that, as a consequence, these specialties are not sharply distinguished from one another? Having no a priori reason for making one or the other of these decisions, we shall tabulate them separately and see how the data fall.

By contrast, the noncommunal specialties may seem to provide a lesser problem. Actually, they too are the sources of some ambiguity in prediction. Let us consider some divergent possibilities. The noncommunal specialties may be only crystallizations of purposes of concern to all members of a sovereign group. Certainly it is plausible to think of hunting or planting or metalworking in those terms. On the other hand, these actions are, by definition, not usually organized as mere instrumentalities of sovereign groups. Instead, while not uninfluenced by sovereign bodies, the people who engage in noncommunal specialties are not governed, in the performance of their specialty, by explicit and particular rules and policies formulated by sovereign organizations. The purposes they pursue tend to be defined socially as those of the specialists themselves, not as those of groups.

Perhaps, however, there is a third possibility. The activities of noncommunal specialists may create special purposes for sovereign groups. This would be the reverse of the relation between sovereign groups and communal specialists. The communal specialist derives his purposes from the group he serves. Perhaps the noncommunal specialist supplies some of the purposes for the groups in which he participates.

To summarize, there are reasons for assuming that the superior gods represent specialized activities. There are, however, no firm grounds for deciding whether they represent communal or noncommunal specialties or both.[3]

FINDINGS

Table V shows the relationship between the number of superior gods and the number of communal specialties. Table VI relates the number of superior gods to the number of noncommunal specialties.

There is a tendency for the number of superior gods to increase with the number of both types of specialties, but the relationship is significantly large ($p = < .05$) only for the number of noncommunal specialties.[4] In interpreting this result, certain other considerations should be examined.

First of all, there may be a kind of bias in these tables. A few of the superior gods enumerated here are directly associated with particular specialties. It may be significant that most of those cases will involve gods of noncommunal spe-

TABLE V

NUMBER OF COMMUNAL SPECIALTIES AND NUMBER OF SUPERIOR GODS

Number of Superior Gods	Number of Communal Specialties	
	One to four	Five or more
Three or more	6	10
One or two	7	5
None	13	7
Total	26	22
Per cent three or more	23	45

TABLE VI

NUMBER OF NONCOMMUNAL SPECIALTIES AND NUMBER OF SUPERIOR GODS

Number of Superior Gods	Number of Noncommunal Specialties	
	None	One or more
Three or more	8	9
One or two	9	3
None	17	3
Total	34	15
Per cent three or more	24	60

cialties, as for example, a god of the blacksmiths or fishermen or carpenters. One is much less likely to find a particular deity for a given communal specialty. True, it is common to find a god of war, but that deity presides over the activities of all participants in battle, not simply the semiprofessional officers who plan or lead the fight. We may get a better understanding of the conditions requisite for a concept of superior gods if we remove those cases of deities explicitly concerned with the activities of only one particular kind of specialist.

When our list of higher gods is purged of such cases, the relationships in our tables change little, but that change is enough to destroy the significant connection between noncommunal specialties and the number of superior deities. It then comes only to the .10 level of probability.

We may, however, try another procedure before concluding that our approach was wrong. It seems reasonable to believe that gods whose actions govern all men engaged in certain activities will be less likely to appear when the ultimately sovereign group is a kinship organization. Why should this be so? An example may help to clarify the point.

Suppose a population's ultimately sovereign group is a clan, phratry, gens, or some other organization based on kinship. As we shall see in the next chapter, the presence of such organizations is associated with a belief in the continued potency of ancestral spirits. This governance of human affairs by the ancestral dead is contrary to the principle of having those affairs controlled by deities associated with a particular activity and with all persons, regardless of their kin relationships, who engage in such action. To the extent that ancestral spirits pre-empt control over human conduct, there is less room for the growth and action of other kinds of spirits. We might expect, then, that there would be a stronger positive association between the number of noncommunal specialties and the number of superior gods in societies lacking ultimately sovereign kinship groups than in those possessing such organizations.

TABLE VII

ULTIMATELY SOVEREIGN KINSHIP GROUPS, NUMBER OF
NONCOMMUNAL SPECIALTIES, AND NUMBER OF SUPERIOR GODS
(OMITTING GODS OF PARTICULAR OCCUPATIONS)

Number of Superior Gods	Ultimately Sovereign Kin Groups Absent		Ultimately Sovereign Kin Groups Present	
	Non-communal Specialties Absent *	Non-communal Specialties Present	Non-communal Specialties Absent *	Non-communal Specialties Present *
Three or more	3	3	3	1
One or two	4	2	3	1
None	9	1	8	2
Total	16	6	14	4
Per cent one or more	44	83	43	50

* Combined for chi-square analysis

Table VII supports this expectation,[5] but, once more, the trend is not significant ($p = < .20$). At this point we are frustrated in two respects. First, we have not found any significant relationship between our purified enumeration of superior gods and the number of specialties in a society. Second, even if such a relationship had appeared, a difficulty would remain. To be specific, we have postulated that spirits symbolize sovereign organizations. An occupational specialty, whether communal or noncommunal, is not such an organization. In the next section of this chapter, an effort to overcome this second source of frustration provides a device for overcoming the first as well. An impression gained from descriptions of primitive societies provides our point of departure.

THE COMPATIBILITY OF SPECIALTIES WITH THE PURPOSES OF GROUPS

A reader of works on primitive societies is likely to sense that communal specialties are particularly fitting expressions of the special purposes of societies in which the ultimately sovereign group is organized on the basis of kinship, that noncommunal specialties are likewise fitting expressions of the purposes of other types of ultimately sovereign groups.[6] At present, no precise statement is available which explains why these varieties of specialization should be more fitting for one type of ultimately sovereign group than another. One can, however, say something of the direction of thinking on the question and present a tabulation which proves consistent with it. The result suggests that our earlier judgment about spirits as symbols of sovereign groups may explain variations in the incidence of superior gods.

Consider first the case in which all of a society's members are bound together in a single, embracive organization founded on descent and marriage—a kinship organization. A man's place in such a society is largely a function of the generation into which he is born, the family into which he marries, and the children he fathers. The major stages in his life involve his succeeding to positions formerly held by parents, grandparents, and great-grandparents. His relationships with other people are determined primarily by their positions as closer or more distant kin. The man who proves outstanding in such a society is one who embodies the group's common values.

Communal and noncommunal specialties differ in their compatibility with a society organized by kinship. The noncommunal specialist—the weaver, the blacksmith, the carpenter—engages in an occupation from which he can obtain influence and wealth apart from that to which his status as a kinsman automatically entitles him. In addition, such specialists develop a web of relationships with other individuals as clients and customers—relationships which are not part of a kinship pattern. Rules of kinship do not determine how people shall interact as buyer and seller and such new factors as the customer's ability to pay and the quality of the seller's product become considerations which may override ties of blood and marriage. In short, the characteristics of a noncommunal specialty bring people into relationships which conflict with bonds of kinship.

By contrast, communal specialties provide lesser difficulties for societies which are structured on the basis of descent and intermarriage. The values of the whole society are expressed by communal specialists—the teacher, the priest, the military leader. These functionaries obtain their influence by expressing the society's customs and purposes, not by virtue of skills which separate them, as individuals, from their kinsmen. Moreover, they serve not customers, but the whole group, and for this reason their specialties are less likely to disrupt that group by evolving new varieties of interpersonal relationships.

There are, of course, societies organized by principles other than kinship which probably find the communal specialties more congenial than the noncommunal. One thinks, for example, of some powerful, but highly legitimate, monarchies and certain theocracies and aristocracies. In each case, the unity of these societies is jeopardized by a proliferation of noncommunal specialists because those specialists can obtain influence, establish personal relationships, and develop values outside the official framework of roles and careers. Apart from societies organized by kinship, our sample of societies contains few or no examples of this variety of organization, and we may simply note that kinship is only a special case of a more general situation.

What of the societies in our sample which are not structured by kinship? In these societies, a man's career is not as likely to consist simply of passage through a series of predetermined roles. There is greater freedom for him to capitalize on personal skills and to employ them in achieving prestige or wealth. There also are fewer barriers to his establishing unascribed relationships with other individuals.

The unity among members of a nonkin society seems founded more on what people do for one another than on who those people are, on performance rather than ascription. This means, in turn, that many of the society's purposes become identical with what people are currently doing for one another, and may change as those services change. In this situation, the rise and decline of noncommunal specialties mirror the shifting interests and purposes of the population and the society. The noncommunal specialties embody many of the society's purposes, while communal specialties, rather than being the conservers and developers of the society's purposes, may become mere administrative conveniences which facilitate the implementation of current purposes.

In the nonkin society, communal specialties are likely to contain real threats to the society's cohesion. Communal specialists often seek to enlarge the scope and powers attached to their roles, to define, and not merely to implement, the population's activities. For this additional reason, such specialists are less suited to express the purposes of nonkin societies.

These admittedly speculative discussions of kin and nonkin societies have implications for the appearance of superior gods. On the hypothesis that superior deities symbolize the special purposes of ultimately sovereign groups, one would conclude that the following relationships should appear.

a. The number of superior gods will be a joint function of the number of specialties in a society and the compatibility of those specialties with the source of the society's purposes.

b. In kin societies, the number of superior gods will be a function of the number of communal specialties.

c. In nonkin societies, the number of superior gods will be a function of the number of noncommunal specialties.

Table VIII shows that such relations appear in our data. Our sample is too small to impose a number of controls on these findings, but the predicted relations appear with strength $(p = < .03)$ sufficient to encourage their further exploration with larger samples. In addition, these results make plausible the judgment that the appearance of superior gods is not a simple function of the number of specialized roles, as such, but of the number of purposes of an ultimately sovereign group which are expressed in *compatible*, specialized roles. If this proves true, the data will be consistent with our theory of spirits as symbols of sovereign groups.

TABLE VIII

NATURE OF ULTIMATELY SOVEREIGN GROUP, NUMBER OF COMMUNAL AND NONCOMMUNAL SPECIALTIES, AND NUMBER OF SUPERIOR GODS (OMITTING GODS OF PARTICULAR OCCUPATIONS)

	Ultimately Sovereign Group							
	Kin Group				Nonkin Group			
	1–4 *		5 or more *		1–4 *		5 or more *	
Number of Superior Gods	1 **′	2 or more **″	1 **′	2 or more **″	1 **′	2 or more **″	1 **′	2 or more **″
Three or more	1	1	2	0	2	0	1	3
One or two	2	0	1	1	2	1	2	1
None	7	2	1	0	3	0	6	1
Total	10	3	4	1	7	1	9	5
Per cent one or more	30	33	75	100	57	100	33	80

* Number of communal specialties
** Number of noncommunal specialties
′, ″ Combined for chi-square analysis

ALTERNATIVE EXPLANATIONS

Because it is evident that we need a much larger sample of societies to provide an adequate test of our explanation of the incidence of superior gods, we shall not discuss the seemingly negative cases from our analysis. It is, in short, too soon to judge which cases are reasonably considered true negatives. We shall, however, note a possible explanation of our results which is somewhat different from the one advanced in this chapter.

In exploring the relations of the number of superior gods to the several remaining social conditions mentioned in Chapter II, we find that the number of such deities relates to the presence of social classes at a point beyond the .05 level of probability.[7] This is the only significant relationship which such an exploration produces. An examination of this new variable as an explanation of our findings must also await studies with larger samples to permit the imposition of appropriate controls.

SUPERIOR GODS OF QUESTIONABLE AUTHENTICITY

What of those named deities whom ethnographers consider important, but whose functions are described so vaguely that we could not give them a definite placement among the superior gods? Tabulations show that the frequency with which they appear is not related to the number of noncommunal specialties. It is significantly and positively connected to two other social conditions: the size of the communities in which the population resides ($p = < .05$) and the number of nonsovereign organizations ($p = < .01$). It is positively, but not quite significantly, related to a third social condition: the number of communal specialties ($p = < .10$). The descriptions of these deities are so poor that we shall not speculate further on the meaning of these findings.

SUMMARY OF RESULTS

1. The number of superior deities is positively and significantly related to the number of specialties of a type compatible with the nature of a society's ultimately sovereign organization.

2. Societies with social classes are significantly more likely than others to possess a belief in superior gods.

3. A much larger sample of societies will be required to explore the complex relations which appear in this chapter.

CHAPTER V

EXPERIENCES WITH ANCESTRAL SPIRITS

Among the supernatural beings known to some primitive and ancient peoples are ancestral spirits. It seems, of course, that all such peoples believe in a life after death. But not all societies possess the idea that the spirits of the dead play some part in the affairs of the living. It now becomes our concern to explain why this is so. In our frame of reference, the problem is one of explaining how the purposes and influence of dead relatives can be experienced as affecting the living.

From one point of view, all living men are influenced by those who went before. The child was instructed and socialized by parents, who, in turn, were reared by their parents, and so back to the beginning of mankind. The chain of influence is almost infinite in its extension through the past. In addition, every man is a product of the wider culture created before his birth by past generations and communicated to him by his community and society as well as by his immediate family. Yet these connections of the living with the dead offer no solution to our problem, for the conduct of all men is influenced by the deeds of forebears, but not all people experience the dead as actively affecting their present behavior.

There are, however, certain features of the active ancestral spirits which suggest an answer to our question. Let us enumerate these characteristics.

First, the active spirits are more than just memories of the dead and more than a generalized tradition which the living acquired from their predecessors. Instead, as individual kinsmen, the deceased enter history once again. Perhaps, as among the Nandi, they come to sip of the beer left for their enjoyment and to play lighthearted pranks on the living. The Nandi smile fondly when they hear the little noises which signal the presence of spirits. But the ancestral dead come to plague and harass the living in some societies, to aid or punish in others. As the ancestors' role grows more important, it is more likely that regular and elaborate ceremonies will be developed through which offerings are made to the dead and their wishes interpreted.

It is significant that these spirits seem to return as members of a kinship system. With such possible exceptions as the ghosts of great leaders or medicine men, the dead contact only those among the living who were related to them or who have some kind of intimacy with remaining members of their kin or with places or affairs of importance to a particular family and its relatives. It tends to be only by accident that persons who are neither related to a ghost nor interacting with his family have contacts with him. It is, therefore, the purposes and influence of the dead in their role as relatives which persist among the living.

We may notice also that, if the returning dead are identified as particular persons among the deceased, as Grandfather So and So or Aunt What's Her Name, they are among the recently departed. The dead, unless very distinguished individuals, are not known by their own names after a generation or two of descendants passes beyond their time. For some of the deceased, this means complete absence from living memories. For some it means attention only as part of a host of revered, but individually unknown, ancestors. In general, then, only the named spirits of the recently departed or exceptionally important dead continue to influence the living.

But why do spirits of the dead return in only some societies? The facts cited thus far provide us with clues.

If the dead typically influence their kin and those associated with their kin, one thinks of their purposes as continuing among the living through some organization of which the deceased were a part and which is also an organization among the members of a particular family. There are two reasons for believing that this organization cannot be the nuclear family, as such. First of all, unions of two or more spouses and their children are universal, or almost so,[1] while belief in active ancestral spirits is not. Second, the nuclear family, as such, is a transitory organization. The children marry and found new households of their own. The parents may live to see their grandchildren and, perhaps, some great-grandchildren, but rarely more. It would be unrealistic to see the nuclear family organization continuing across the generations and, through it, the purposes of the dead.

Just as we have searched for particular groups as the source of those experiences from which there spring beliefs in high gods or polytheistic deities, so we now search for social organizations which will embody the influence of dead ancestors, and which, unlike the nuclear family, will carry on the purposes of the deceased in seeming perpetuity.

We shall expect to find active ancestral spirits in societies which have kinship organizations more embracive than the nuclear family, organizations that continue to embody the purposes which, as former members of these groups, the ancestors shared. The procedure employed will be a count of all kinship organizations—gentes, kindreds, lineages, clans, phratries, moieties, and all the rest—which, in a given society, are also sovereign groups.

But this prediction may have to be qualified for a certain kind of situation. When a sovereign kinship group other than the nuclear family is also the society's ultimately sovereign group, a new principle may enter to modify our expectations.

Ultimately sovereign groups must engage in the governing of a territory. Their members and constituents are certain to relate to one another as persons who reside in a common territory and exploit such resources as space, arable land, game, fish, and the like. Whether or not these people are kin, they will have relationships which arise, not directly from the fact of kinship, but from their occupancy of a common territory. An ultimately sovereign group must develop means of allocating and commandeering resources such as dance grounds, water, arable land, pasturage, streets, weapons, and such others as are required to permit the continuation of a population residing in a particular area. It must define membership, establish tests of admission, devise means for settling disputes, provide for leisure activities, and strengthen collective loyalties. Many of these activities may be conducted by members of a kinship organization, but these responsibilities are not outgrowths of the kin dependencies, but of the interrelations which people share because they are geographically close and because they are members of the same community or the same district or kingdom.

As we have seen, dead relatives return to their roles as members of a kin group. But the ancestor was not only a possessor of the purposes which that group perpetuates. In a very special sense, he made possible the participation in those purposes by some among the living. To make this clear, we may contrast the role of the ancestor with that of the headman of a primitive village. Only one person is headman at a particular period in a village's history, but he usually did not create this post or its policies. He is an incumbent, not an originator. Parents, however, by procreation, make it possible for their offspring to live and hence to become eligible for membership in a kinship group. The parents, as the origin of children and, through them, of grandchildren, are creators as well as occupants of kin relations. The rules of biological and social procreation are such that only one particular person can be a man's paternal grandfather and only a few can be his maternal uncles. Individual and role are indissolubly linked in a way which is not prevalent when we consider nonkin relationships. Hence, as individuals, the dead who are not one's relatives may fail to live along with their roles although ancestors do.

The few cases in which departed individuals, who are not also members of one's family line, are believed active in the affairs of the living underscore the points just made. Those individuals, real or imagined, tend to be associated with the creation of a new and important role: the culture heroes who brought fire, magic, weapons, or other vital gifts to the people; the real or mythical first ancestors of the society; the headman who was associated with a tribe's expansion from a sleepy little village to a vast empire. Interestingly, such persons are honored by the complex as well as the simpler societies, and their influence is spoken of as persisting through the ages.

When a kinship group is identical in personnel with the population's ultimately sovereign organization, a difficulty appears. As members of such a kinship group the ancestors would presumably be active in the lives of living descendants. However, as predecessors in the territorial unit, there may not be a basis for such activity. Since the individual ancestor is welded to his kin role, and it to him, he may not be divisible. We must, therefore, consider that this dual function of the deceased who are predecessors in nonkin roles and also ancestors, may inhibit a belief in their continued activity among the living.[2] For that reason, we shall make no prediction for cases in which the ultimately sovereign unit is a kinship group, and shall tabulate such instances separately.

We shall classify the activities of dead ancestors in our sample into four categories. There are some cases in which the observers do not report that the dead influence the living. There are situations in which the deceased's influence is portrayed in such vague terms as bringing misfortune or playing pranks, but not further described. There are societies in which the departed aid or punish their descendants, implying that the living merit this assistance or punishment. Finally, we find societies in which the dead are invoked by their descendants. In this fourth case, the descendants have some claim upon, or power over, the deceased relatives which they can exercise to guide the actions of the dead.

FINDINGS

Table IX shows the relationship we expected between active ancestral spirits and the presence of sovereign kinship groups (other than the nuclear family and ultimately sovereign organizations). Only three of the 23 societies with such kinship groups lack active ancestrals. Half of the 24 societies without such kinship groups possess active ancestral spirits. This finding is significant beyond the .01 level of probability. The association between these variables produces a coefficient of contingency of .33, which, when corrected, becomes .47.

TABLE IX

SOVEREIGN KINSHIP GROUPS (OTHER THAN NUCLEAR FAMILIES AND ULTIMATELY SOVEREIGN GROUPS) AND THE ACTIVITY OF ANCESTRAL SPIRITS

Ancestral Spirits	Sovereign Kinship Groups	
	Absent	Present
Are invoked	3	11
Aid or punish	4	6
Active	5	3
Inactive	12	3
Total	24	23
Per cent active in some fashion	50	87

No relationship appears between the presence of ultimately sovereign kinship groups and the activity of dead ancestors. Table X adds the presence of these sovereign kinship groups to the cases of Table IX to show their combined relationship to a belief in active ancestrals. Once again, the association is positive and significant. The result is significant beyond the .03 level of probability. One society of the 11 with at least two sovereign kinship groups lacks active ancestrals. Less than a fifth of the 11 societies with one such group do not also evidence a belief in the activity of dead kin. There are, however, eight of the 17 societies without

TABLE X

SOVEREIGN KINSHIP GROUPS (OTHER THAN NUCLEAR FAMILIES) AND THE ACTIVITY OF ANCESTRAL SPIRITS

	Number of Sovereign Kinship Groups		
Ancestral Spirits	0	1	2 or more
Are invoked	2	4	6
Aid or punish	2	4	2
Active	4	1	2
Inactive	9	2	1
Total	17	11	11
Per cent active in some fashion	47	82	91

sovereign kin groups who possess such a belief. These eight cases, together with the Aztec who have two sovereign kin groups and lack a belief in active ancestral spirits, now engage our attention.

NEGATIVE EVIDENCE

The eight societies that clearly fail to meet our expectations are the Arunta, Carib, Copper Eskimo, Karen, Lozi, Marquesan, Yahgan and Yokuts. Three of these, the Arunta, Marquesan, and Yokuts, may involve misclassification.

We are told that the Arunta of central Australia have a totem center in each local settlement. These settlements are the ultimately sovereign units. Further, the Arunta believe that souls go to a totemic storehouse from which they are reborn. The local leader is described as a totem chief. These facts are important because it is not uncommon for a totemic system to be accompanied by the belief that all persons in the group are in some sense descendants of the totem objects, whether a plant, animal, or something else. Unfortunately, there is no unambiguous statement in our sources that such ancestry is part of Arunta totemism. If it were, we should have to reclassify the local settlements as sovereign kinship groups. The data are too ambiguous, however, to justify such a move.[3]

The Marquesans, an island people in the southern Pacific, may also be misclassified. Marquesan "tribes" consist of nuclear households which keep genealogical records extending back for sixty to eighty generations. These people also regard all tribal members as having a common ancestor. Perhaps this signifies that they consider their society to be a kinship organization. The evidence is unclear.

Turning to the Yokuts of California, we find the statement by Alfred Kroeber [4] that they are organized into "true" tribes. Now the word "tribe" is indeed slippery. It can mean any aggregate of primitives who have a common name and culture. It can be used to designate those who live within a particular ultimately sovereign group. Finally, there are several more technical meanings. Kroeber tells me,[5] however, that the Yokuts' tribes were not kin groups. Thus they do not fit our prediction.

In the five remaining cases, no such possibilities of misclassification have come to light. Further, no alternative explanations appear which might account for their exceptional status. The Aztec must also be added to our list of exceptions. Aztec clans were sovereign groups and the ultimately sovereign organization of their society—the tribe—appears to have been a kinship unit. Yet there seems to be no firm evidence of a belief in active ancestral spirits. Later research should pay special attention to these six cases and the Yokuts.

ALTERNATIVE EXPLANATIONS

One might ask whether the presence in many societies of kinship classifications which are not sovereign might relate to the activity of ancestral spirits. For example, many societies have such kinship aggregations as moieties or clans or phratries. These may not be present as groups, that is, their members or the members' representatives do not meet to do business as a particular social unit. On the other hand, these classifications affect behavior. Frequently a person must marry within or outside such a category. There may be other rules which prescribe special responsibilities for members toward one another. Some such aggregations customarily play particular roles in ceremonies or compete with one another in games. In addition, there are societies in which these kin categories are organized as nonsovereign groups.

We have rejected such unorganized and nonsovereign aggregations as models of active ancestral spirits because their status as purposing agencies is in doubt. Either, as among the unorganized kin categories, the aggregation as such does not make decisions and choices, or, as among the nonsovereign kin groups, the group's purposes are likely to be experienced as originating outside these organizations.

These judgments are supported by the data. Table XI shows that no relationship exists between such kin aggregates and the activity of dead relatives.

TABLE XI

UNORGANIZED KINSHIP CATEGORIES, NONSOVEREIGN KINSHIP GROUPS, AND THE ACTIVITY OF ANCESTRAL SPIRITS

Ancestral Spirits	Unorganized Kinship Categories or Non-sovereign Kinship Groups	
	Absent	Present
Are invoked	12	2
Aid or punish	7	4
Active	6	2
Inactive	12	3
Total	37	11
Per cent active in some fashion	68	73

Since the number of sovereign kinship groups is part of the total number of a society's sovereign organizations, we might wonder whether the latter is related to ancestral spirits' activity. The answer is negative.

Finally, we may note that no alternative explanation of the activity of ancestrals has come to hand. Sumner and Keller [6] propose that men develop the notion that the dead still exist because they are seen in dreams. This might help to explain the almost universal idea that men have souls which continue to live in an afterworld. It does not seem relevant, however, to account for differences among societies in the extent to which dead ancestors participate in human affairs.

SUMMARY OF RESULTS

1. There is a positive and significant relationship between the presence in a society of sovereign kinship groups other than the nuclear family and a belief that ancestral spirits are active in human affairs.

2. There is no relationship between the presence or number of unorganized or nonsovereign kinship aggregations in a society and the activity of ancestral spirits.

CHAPTER VI

REINCARNATION

Of all the beliefs which Western ethnographers describe in other cultures, few seem more exotic to them than a faith in reincarnation. Perhaps the setting which reincarnation has in India, complete with the idea of the Wheel of Life and the blissfully vacuous Nirvana, stimulates this impression of strangeness. Perhaps its sharp difference from the fundamentals of Western religion and science makes reincarnation appear so bizarre.

This chapter examines the concept of reincarnation and presents an explanation for its appearance. The explanation is tested against evidence from our sample of the simpler societies.

In all cases of reincarnation, the dead are said to return to life. Once again they feel and grow, they age, learn, desire and suffer. In most cases, they return as personalities. Their old selves are identifiable. The traits they possessed earlier still characterize their behavior. True, if the reborn comes as an infant, he must learn again the ways of adults, but his new parents and neighbors may recognize in the shape of his hands, the expression of his face, or his temperament, the original being who once more assumes a corporal existence. The soul or spirit has, in some sense, continued to have the identity it possessed in a previous life. It is the flesh which is drastically changed.

There are, however, a few cases in which a kind of reincarnation occurs without seeming to preserve this continuity of personality. In our sample, the Karen illustrate this point. The observer of their beliefs tells us that they do not seem to conceive of an immortal life. The Karen souls, once in the afterworld, die, or perhaps more accurately, become immobile and vegetative. In the latter form they swell until, bursting over the fields, they fertilize the rice. When the grain is eaten, this life-giving fluid enables men and animals to reproduce. In any case, the soul or animating principle of the individual continues its work in new living bodies and even enables those bodies to reproduce their kind.

How can such beliefs be explained? How can the purposes of a dead individual continue to live in nature and affect its course? We have just seen that the dead, while retaining their supernatural status as disembodied spirits, may be active in human affairs if a continuing kinship group exists in their society. But this differs from reincarnation in that the ancestral spirits do not assume corporal form and the dead return as ancestors, not in their other roles.

Following the reasoning of the last chapter, we shall assume that if the dead are still active in human affairs, there must be some organization which continues to exist and which embodies their purposes. But this is too general a formula to explain reincarnation. We must go further and say how the influences of particular individuals can be perpetuated—if not forever, then at least for a generation or two beyond their death—and how this can be if the dead do not continue active solely in their role as kin but assume once more the whole round of human life.

We find a hint in those situations where the spirit of

some person other than an ancestor is believed to intervene in nature and especially in human society. As we saw in the preceding chapter, these people are distinguished because they had unusual influence on their fellows when they were alive. They are such persons as outstanding warriors, statesmen, inventors, and medicine men. These individuals are believed responsible for important and persisting characteristics of the social world.

But what of the less spectacular members of a society? When might their influence as particular individuals continue after they die? When do the purposes which they, as individuals, held become so vital that they continue after the flesh which possessed them is buried?

We know from studies in our own society and from common observation that the influence of most individuals is greatest within their own families and among their close friends. As we have noted, however, these little groups are short-lived. For that reason, among others, we rejected them as providing the continuity required for the activity of dead ancestors. How can they serve us now?

Let us suppose that a small cluster of related nuclear families or a tiny community of unrelated households lived in relative isolation from its neighbors. Suppose, further, that the adults in these few families share much of life in common: hunting together, planting a common field or herding their cattle in a joint enterprise, perhaps having a common table. Or, as an alternative, imagine, again in such relative isolation, a large polygynous or polyandrous household, in which the father and his wives or the mother and her several husbands work as a unit. These small groups are a kind of world of their own. If they follow the patterns noted in many studies,[1] they develop private jokes and unique patterns of work. Within them, the individual and his peculiarities are of much interest and importance. Being rather isolated, these groups must depend on the current pattern of tastes and temperaments and skills of their members in making a living and in reaching decisions. They do not find it easy to go outside for new resources. The particular potentialities of each member are appreciated as limiting or facilitating the lives of all the others, and those effects persist after a member dies—his technological inventiveness, his habit of shirking work, his fecundity, or the qualities of his voice in the ceremonial songs have shaped adaptations of his fellows which continue after his death.

The small and rather isolated settlement has two other properties relevant for our purpose. First, it has a continuity which ordinary nuclear families lack. In many cases, a community of such families, however tiny its population, will continue, as a community, through time although its nuclear families change through death and through the marriage of the grown children. In other cases, as that of the polygynous household, the enlarged family is also a community, and some or all of its members are likely to remain as residents of the same land or as shepherds of the common herds despite the changes of personnel brought by migration, demise of the father, or marriage.

Second, the influence of an individual in some such situations clearly extends to areas of experience which are not ordered by kinship. These are groups founded on a territorial principle as well as on the local rules of kinship. As the preceding chapter stated, relationships may arise among their members which spring, not directly from the fact of kinship, but from their common occupancy of the same territory. We may suppose that the individual's continuing influence in these circumstances extends beyond his kinship roles to his impact as a neighbor and fellow inhabitant.

Up to this point, we have pictured a situation in which the purposes of particular individuals may be perpetuated for a generation or more after their death in the affairs of very small and rather isolated communities. This speculative account must now be elaborated at one important point.

The kind of situation just described may be found in large as well as small societies. Because the tiny community is isolated and fairly self-sufficient, it is not necessarily the ultimately sovereign organization to which its members give allegiance. To the contrary, we shall find that such a pattern of hamlets and family compounds is the standard form of settlement within many large chiefdoms and kingdoms as well as in smaller populations.

Finally, we must make a special tabulation of three societies in our sample. In each of these cases—the Shoshoni, Yahgan, and Yurok—the nuclear family is the ultimately sovereign unit. Since such families are highly transitory groups, we shall expect that their presence as ultimately sovereign units will *not* be associated with a belief in reincarnation.

To summarize, we anticipate that reincarnation is likely to appear where the pattern of settlement is by small hamlets, compounds of extended families, small nomadic bands, scattered rural neighborhoods, or other units smaller than a village. These are the smallest units of settlement described in Chapter II. The exception to this expectation will be the nuclear family whose household is also the ultimately sovereign group.

FINDINGS

Table XII provides confirmation for our expectations. Reincarnation is significantly more likely to appear in the small units described above than in any other type of settlement. The significance level of this finding is beyond .01. The coefficient of contingency is .37, which, when corrected for the number of cells in the computation, becomes .52.

TABLE XII

UNIT OF SETTLEMENT AND REINCARNATION

	Unit of Settlement			
Reincarnation	Nuclear Household *	Neighborhoods, etc.	Villages	Towns or Cities
Present	0	9	3	1
Absent	3	8	19	7
Total	3	17	22	8
Per cent present	0	53	14	13

* Is ultimately sovereign group

NEGATIVE EVIDENCE

There are, however, a number of cases which do not meet our initial expectations. Eight societies lack a belief in rebirth under conditions which we felt would produce such a belief. They are Arapesh, Aymara, Blackfoot, Ifaluk, Ifugao,

Tallensi, Tiv, and Yagua. Four societies—the Ga, Karen, Lengua, and Winnebago—possess reincarnation beliefs contrary to our expectation. Let us see whether the records suggest why these exceptions occurred.

A suggestion from Chapter V may help us here. In the discussion of experiences with ancestral spirits, we argued that a conflict between a man's roles as ancestor and as predecessor in a territorial unit might lessen the chances that ancestral spirits would be perceived as active in human affairs. We judged that this conflict of roles might be especially likely when the ultimately sovereign territorial unit was also organized as a kinship group. The data of Chapter V did not give unambiguous support to the notion that ancestral spirits would be less likely to play an active role in the affairs of the living under such conditions.

Suppose, however, that something like the reverse were true. Suppose that, when a society's ultimately sovereign group is organized along kinship lines, the chances decline that a dead man has contacts with the living in any role other than that of an ancestral spirit.

Retabulation (see Table XIII) provides enough support for this possibility to suggest that it is worthy of further exploration and elaboration with new data compiled especially for that purpose. Of the eight cases in which reincarnation beliefs fail to occur among societies settled under the category "Neighborhoods, etc." in Table XII, six are instances in which the ultimately sovereign group is a kinship organization. By contrast, three of the nine societies that lie in that category of settlement and possess beliefs in reincarnation also have kinship units as their ultimately sovereign groups.

TABLE XIII

ULTIMATELY SOVEREIGN KINSHIP GROUPS, UNIT OF
SETTLEMENT AND REINCARNATION

| | Ultimately Sovereign Kinship Groups | | | | | | | |
| | Present | | | | Absent | | | |
Reincarnation	NH *	N *	V *	T *	NH *	N *	V *	T *
Present	0	3	1	0	0	4	1	1
Absent	3	6	2	2	0	2	13	4
Total	3	9	3	2	0	6	14	5
Per cent present	0	33	33	0	0	67	7	20

* Unit of settlement: NH—nuclear family's household
　　　　　　　　　　 N—neighborhoods, et al.
　　　　　　　　　　 V—villages
　　　　　　　　　　 T—towns or cities

We may look, as well, at the four cases of societies not classified under "Neighborhoods, etc.," which lack ultimately sovereign kinship groups and exhibit a belief in rebirth. The Karen hill people of Burma are the first to engage our attention.

The Karen were mentioned earlier in this chapter as believing in a kind of reincarnation in which souls of the dead burst over the rice, fertilizing it and imparting, through the rice, reproductive powers to men and animals. This belief was called reincarnation because the dead are perpetuated in new, living bodies. Perhaps, however, the soul's loss of identity should have been given greater consideration. Unlike most other cases in our classification, the native cannot say which of the dead has returned. Further, the soul does not retain its original personality, but enters the lives of others in fragments of fertilizing material. In short, this case

may not fulfill our requirement that the purposes of a particular deceased individual, as such, continue to play a role in
the activities of the living.

Next to claim our attention are the Lengua bands who
live along the western bank of the Paraguay River. The most
detailed account of their culture appears in the work of
W. Barbrooke Grubb, an Anglican missionary, who spent
23 years among them. The ethnographer's background is of
importance in this instance because, first, his report seems
objective and quite understanding of native life and, second,
his clerical training enables him to be more precise and
elaborate about supernatural matters than might otherwise
be true.

Grubb speaks [2] of the Lengua as having an "indistinct"
belief in reincarnation. The idea is that souls sometimes seek
rebirth by entrance into the world as newborn infants.
Grubb stresses that these efforts are only occasional and not
always successful. The older soul must oust the spirit which
would normally belong to the child at birth. Perhaps, as in
the case of the Karen, we should see this as a less convincing
instance of reincarnation than those of other societies. It
does, however, meet our formal criteria as related earlier in
this chapter.

By contrast, the Ga people, now incorporated into the
newly independent nation of Ghana, and the Winnebago
Indians of Wisconsin may be genuine exceptions to our
expectation. Both appear to have well developed beliefs in
reincarnation and neither seems to have a social structure
which, according to our prediction, should give rise to a
conception of rebirth. Unfortunately, no obvious alternative

explanation comes to hand which might account for these divergent cases.

ALTERNATIVE EXPLANATIONS

A search of the literature has not unearthed any alternative account to the one given here. Further, none of the remaining indicators of social conditions employed in these chapters is related to the presence of reincarnation.

A NOTE ON REINCARNATION IN INDIA

Having proposed an explanation for the concept of rebirth and having gained support for that hypothesis from a sample of ancient and primitive peoples, one naturally asks whether the same explanation will fit the case of India. Brahmanism teaches that the essential soul (*atma*) of the individual, although not his entire personality, finds a new corporal existence when the old body dies. It states further that the earthly fate or lot (*karma*) of the newly born individual depends upon the character, values, and, in particular, the fulfillment or nonfulfillment of caste-duty (*dharma*) of the person in whom the soul was previously incarnate. Thus, if a man lives evilly or fails in his caste-dharma in this life, he will be reincarnated as a lower caste person or even as an animal in one or more future births. If he lives virtuously and fulfills his caste-duty admirably, he will be reborn in a higher caste or (if he is already of the highest, Brahmanical, caste) in the same caste as before. Brahman intellectuals look forward to the time when, after very many rebirths, having cast from their souls all interest in and commerce with finite affairs, the chain of rebirth ends, and the soul becomes one with the ineffable spirit of Brahman.[3] The theory of rebirth is especially significant in formulating the relations between castes. It seems to be held weakly or not at all by the lower castes.

Existing literature does not seem to contain any explanations of Brahman reincarnation. Further, an examination of the settlement pattern of the Indian population shows that most natives live in communities which we would have classified as villages or towns, not as the tiny residential units associated with reincarnation in our sample of primitives.

There is, however, one facet of Indian village life which may provide conditions similar to those we have linked to the idea of rebirth. It is the existence of castes—priests, potters, agriculturalists, weavers, and all the rest. Apparently, the caste system is at least as old as reincarnation in Indian life. The members of each caste perform special and essential services for the rest of the community. The Indian village is an organic whole in which caste specialists work together to shape a common life. But this is not the entire story. Members of any particular caste tend to live near one another. As participants in the tasks and obligations of a special caste, they join one another in the ritual observances attendant upon their social status. A man marries within his caste and collaborates with other caste members in performing their particular service to village life. Together with members of his caste, he meets to discuss the problems and conditions of the caste's work. Thus, united by work and marriage and by the decisions which the caste's local council makes for its members, and separated by sacred proscriptions from members of other castes, the personnel of a particular caste in a particular village constitutes something like a separate community.[4]

It would not be unusual, for example, for a village of 800 persons to contain 35 castes. Averaged out, this would give each caste about 23 members. It may be, then, that in these small, organized, continuing, and semisegregated castes, we have a structure which fulfills the requirements set in this chapter for generating a belief in rebirth.

SUMMARY OF RESULTS

1. Reincarnation is positively and significantly related to a settlement pattern of neighborhoods, nomadic bands, extended family compounds, and other small, but continuing, units.

2. Such settlement patterns may be found in societies which differ widely in population.

3. Although requiring a great deal of further exploration, it is plausible that when such units of settlement are present, reincarnation beliefs will not appear if the ultimately sovereign group in the population is organized according to kinship principles.

4. The belief in rebirth associated with Brahmanism may or may not be associated with small, but continuing, units of settlement. Available data are inconclusive.

CHAPTER VII

THE IMMANENCE OF THE SOUL

We have searched for those experiences of purpose which give rise to conceptions of high gods, polytheistic deities, active ancestral spirits, and reincarnation. In each instance we have made some progress toward an answer. In each we are left with certain unexplained cases. But the perspective employed in all of the predictions made and tested up to this point may help us to account for yet another difference among societies. This is the difference in belief in the immanence of the soul.

Whatever else it represents, the word "soul" refers to an individual's characteristic skills, motives, and capacities. They are the resources which he brings to his relations with the environment and through which his behavior toward that environment is developed. These traits, or some of them, lie behind specific behaviors, guiding and shaping their course, but not fully revealed by any one of the individual's acts. They form a body of resources, organized and available, from which a person may draw in meeting the environment and living in it.

This body of potentialities, invisible and known only through its consequences, is commonly considered as somehow different from the body. The body perishes, but the soul is immortal. It is the animating principle—sometimes the actual cause—of life, of thinking, willing, and knowing.

The simpler societies differ in the degree to which body

and soul are separated. In some, the soul is a substance inherent or immanent in the body. It may go free when the body dies, but, while the living body endures, the soul is conceived as lodged in the flesh. People in certain other societies appear to think of the soul as transcendent in relation to the body. In such cases, the soul, or spirit, of a man directs his flesh but definitely is not of it.

The existence of differences in belief about the immanence of the soul is inferred from some of the facts of primitive ideology. It may be derived from the presence or absence of such practices as exuvial magic, cannibalism, and the taking of the scalp, head, or other parts of an enemy's body. How may these practices and the ideas related to them be connected to the notion of immanence?

Exuvial magic employs products of a man's body to control his behavior. The sorcerer collects nail parings, excrement, spittle, blood, hair, semen, or bits of skin from the man he wants to influence. Such substances are an essential ingredient in his magic. As he manipulates them, so he can manipulate his subject's conduct.

It is evident that there is no direct, material connection between boiling a man's blood and causing him to fall ill, or a preparation made from his hair and his choice of a lover. The sorcerer believes, however, that a supernatural realm connects his magical practices with his objectives. In a man's blood, spittle, or other exuviae resides some of his essential substance—some of his soul—and control over the part gives some control over the remainder. This is the kind of rationale which we have interpreted as a description of the immanence of the soul in the body.

A similar rationale usually underlies the taking of scalps

or heads or the eating of an enemy's flesh. A report, like Linton's,[1] that the Marquesans ate their dead foe because they liked the flavor of human meat, is indeed rare. The usual reason for these customs lies in the belief that, by owning or ingesting part of a man, one gains his services or his talents. The belief of some primitives that killing or eating a lion imparts the beast's strength, stealth, stamina, lordliness, or courage typically rests on the same conception. True, the warrior who takes a scalp may receive no benefit from his deed until, when he dies, he has his victim as a slave in the afterlife, but the principle appears to be the same. By owning or controlling a part of a man's body, one gets the benefit of that man's powers and potentialities. In fact, among some peoples, scalps and heads can be transferred, even sold, and the recipient of the gift or the purchase falls heir to supernatural benefits attached to these human remains. Likewise, it is not uncommon that such rewards go to all who eat of an enemy's corpse, not just to the person who killed the foeman.

It might be thought that the practice of human sacrifice similarly implies an idea of a soul immanent in the flesh. That, however, seems doubtful. Despite the presence of human flesh in the sacrifice and despite the benefits received by the worshippers, instances of human sacrifice differ from the others we have mentioned in one crucial respect. There is no conception in the sacrifice that the dead man's flesh will be used to control his conduct or that his death will give his powers and abilities to those who killed him. It is, therefore, not an association between his body and soul that is exploited, but his suitability as a gift for the spirits.

But, supposing all the foregoing to be true, under what circumstances might we expect the soul to be thought immanent in the body, in what circumstances transcendent? Let us consider the meaning of "soul" in more detail.

The idea of a man's spirit or soul, his animating principle, has features in common with concepts like personality or motives or abilities and attitudes. As we know, all of these psychological concepts refer to potentialities or predispositions which may be idiosyncratic to the individual or shared widely by those around him. If, for example, we meet a young matron who feels sympathetic toward a crying child or who is interested in new fashions in clothing, we assume that she has acquired these tastes in her role as a woman. If, on the other hand, she has always had a particular liking for the color red or if she cannot tolerate the slightest joke at her expense, we quickly turn for an explanation to some unique experiences she has had. This is probably a reasonable decision, since her preference for red and her aversion to humor aimed at her person are not obvious characteristics of any commonly recognized groups or roles in our population.

Those features of a person's "soul" which are produced by the social roles and the groups in which he lives, are not readily seen as his alone. Such motives and attitudes and abilities continue to exist as long as others are socialized as he was. These aspects of his conduct have, therefore, a life beyond his own and origins other than in experiences peculiar to a given individual.

Any of a man's major interests or abilities or purposes might have been acquired from a group. Every characteristic of the individual which has such an origin is partially independent of his person, is "lodged" outside his body. If we assume that each group to which a man belongs is the unique source of distinctive characteristics which the individual acquires, then, other things being equal, we may predict that the greater the number of organized groups to which a society's members belong, the more likely will it be that their spirits will not be considered immanent in their bodies. How may this prediction be tested?

Our enumeration of the sovereign groups in a society provides one list of organized groups to which all members belong. It is not complete, and the published descriptions of societies in our sample are not generally adequate to produce a comprehensive tabulation. On the other hand, the list of sovereign groups does enumerate those to which *all* persons in the society belong. Were we to count groups subsidiary to these, we should risk including many in which only some or a very few of a society's people have membership. We must recognize, therefore, that our indicator of the number of organized groups to which people belong is gross. It must suffice until further empirical and theoretical work clarifies the nature of a more adequate measure.

Now we turn to social conditions which might be expected to interact with the number of sovereign groups as the latter relates to immanence of soul. We shall consider three such conditions: intimate but unlegitimated contacts, unit of settlement, and the presence of sovereign kinship organizations.

UNLEGITIMATED CONTACTS

First, then, what of intimate but unlegitimated contacts? These are situations in which people must interact closely with one another for the achievement of common ends. In this respect they are intimate. In addition, these are situations in which the relations among people were not developed with the consent, tacit or explicit, of all concerned; or in which persons with conflicting objectives cannot resolve their differences through commonly agreed upon means such as the courts or community councils.

Such situations indicate the weakening of a society's unity. We shall expect that a man's spirit is more likely to be associated with his body under these conditions than would be the case if he belonged to a more integrated society. Among the peoples in our sample, there are two types of situation which fit this general description of intimate interaction in the absence of public and legitimate devices for settling grievances or compromising conflicts of purpose.

One of these situations exists when the members of one society must have very close and intimate relations with those of another. It is not uncommon, for example, for the people of one village to have rules which require that they marry outside the community. Let us suppose that these rules are present together with the condition that each village is the ultimately sovereign group for its members. The consequence is that men must obtain wives from groups to which they, themselves, do not belong. In those alien groups they sometimes are not protected by laws or customary rules or public practices which define their rights and protect their interests. Further, it is almost inevitable that such nearby communities will have some conflicting interests such as competition for scarce land or water or game. As a consequence, men who go courting will have to deal with women, and with the kin and neighbors of women, who have important objectives at variance with their own.

The prescription of joint rituals and ceremonies between members of different ultimately sovereign organizations has similar implications. Consider, for example, rules which state that valid worship of the spirits or the valid initiation of the young cannot occur unless the adults from several adjacent societies are present. The fruits of worship or initiation are of great importance. Yet one must depend on appropriate actions by aliens to achieve such goals. These strangers, uncontrolled by the customs and opinions of one's own group, play an essential role in making one's children into full adult citizens and in relating the interests of one's society to the actions of the supernatural. Will such aliens play their part to one's benefit or, since their interests may well conflict with those of one's own society, will they exploit the situation for their own ends? Further, can they be trusted to behave peaceably and helpfully when members of the several societies meet?

The second type of situation in which a society's integration is weakened arises when, within the confines of a sovereign group, there are important and persistent conflicts among members which are not capable of just resolution through publicly supported means. Take, for instance, the cases in which one clan or tribe has conquered several others, welding them by force into a single kingdom and exercising continued domination over the conquered. Since the simpler peoples usually lack the kind of embracive economy which binds conquerer and conquered into a single national system of trade and production, thus gradually obliterating the sharper differences between ruler and ruled, it is to be expected that both superordinate and subject peoples will try to control each other in the absence of legitimate public means. This is, at best, an uneasy relationship.

It is further typical of primitive empires assembled by conquest that no effective means has been found to provide orderly succession to high positions in government. Wars of succession are common. Rebellion against the present ruler is always in the air. People's loyalties are not firmly rooted in commitments to one stable regime.[2]

Another example of this second type of situation occurs when, for whatever reason, powerful and conflicting groups in the same society make demands on the same individuals without providing legitimate means for resolving these conflicts. The Navaho provide a case in point. A man is considered duty bound to aid his own parents and siblings, to take their side in disputes. At the same time, he is required to live with his wife's family and to assist in its projects. The frequent result is that he is torn between the interests of the two groups while his wife finds it hard to reconcile differences of interest between her own blood relatives and her husband.

We shall expect the weakening of a society's integration where members of two or more ultimately sovereign groups are said to intermarry frequently or to hold common ceremonies. We do not count as intimate relations the important, but rather less personal, contacts involved in trade or occasional alliance in war. We shall also anticipate that a society will be less integrated when it is an enforced union of conquered peoples or when, as among the Navaho, married partners are reported to have strong conflicts of interest between their original family and that of their spouse or when, for whatever reason, strong and persistent conflicts of interest exist between husband and wife. In this latter connection, we shall not include cases of frequent divorce or separation said to be generated by causes other than conflicts of persistent and important interests. Finally, we shall expect impaired integration whenever the ethnographer reports that there are severe and unresolvable conflicts between persons who occupy different and widespread social roles in a society and when the nature of those diverse roles is the source of the conflict among their occupants. A case in point would be that of the Nyakyusa among whom the interests of older and younger men are violently opposed—the younger need their seniors' wealth to buy wives and the older seek to keep that wealth in order to add to the number of their own wives. Further, Nyakyusa custom lets all of a man's brothers inherit his property. They must all die before his sons can get anything. As a result the older men have a privileged position which inherently frustrates the interests of their sons and nephews.

UNIT OF SETTLEMENT

The chapters on reincarnation and ancestral spirits also contribute to our present work. Since reincarnation, like immanence of soul, implies that the individual's powers are his own rather than those of some group, the small units of settlement associated with a belief in rebirth should also be associated with head-hunting, exuvial magic, cannibalism, and the taking of scalps.

SOVEREIGN KINSHIP ORGANIZATIONS

By contrast, the presence of sovereign kinship organizations should inhibit a conception of immanent souls. Such organizations foster a belief in active ancestral spirits and, in their turn, the existence of such spirits implies that the powers of particular individuals flow, not from themselves, but from membership in kin groups. Kinship organizations should be uniquely potent in this respect precisely because they do connect *particular individuals* to unique social roles. This point was elaborated in Chapter V.

PLAN OF ANALYSIS

The plan of analysis will require cross-classifying our 50 societies by the four conditions described above and assigning weights to each condition according to its expected relationship to immanence of soul. This means, for example, that we shall attach a weight of one to societies having two or fewer sovereign groups since the absence of such groups is expected to have a positive relation to immanence. Because the presence of such groups is expected to show a negative relation to immanence of soul, it receives a weight of zero. (See condition and weight table on page 131.)

We shall expect that the likelihood of finding immanence of soul will increase as the number of forces evocative of that conception increases. This will mean a positive relationship between the total weight assigned a society and the probability that it possesses exuvial magic, head-hunting, scalp-taking, or cannibalism.

Social Condition		*Weight*
Number of sovereign groups	Two or fewer	1
	Three or more	0
Unlegitimated contacts	Present	1
	Absent	0
Small, continuing settlements *	Present	1
	Absent	0
Sovereign kinship groups	Present	0
	Absent	1

* The word "continuing" requires a weight of zero for societies in which the nuclear household is the ultimately sovereign group. The rationale for this was presented in the chapter on reincarnation.

FINDINGS

Table XIV shows that our data support this expectation. To clarify its information, Table XV is also given. Of the 18 societies with weights of zero or one, 14 lack evidence for a belief in immanence of soul. Six of the nine societies with weights of three or four exhibit such evidence. This trend is significant at a point beyond the .01 level of probability. Inspection of Table XIV also shows that the interaction of the four social conditions produces our finding. Taken by itself, not one is related significantly to immanence.

TABLE XIV

SELECTED SOCIAL RELATIONS AND IMMANENCE OF SOUL

Immanence of Soul	Category *																
	1	2	3	4	5	6	7	8	9	10	11	12	13	14	15	16	x
Present	2	1	1	2	1	1	2	0	3	1	3	1	1	0	0	4	0
Absent	2	0	2	0	3	0	6	2	1	0	1	2	0	0	1	0	3
Total	4	1	3	2	4	1	8	2	4	1	4	3	1	0	1	4	3
Total weight	2	3	1	2	1	2	0	1	3	4	2	3	2	3	1	2	2

* Sovereign groups: Two or less: 9–16   Three or more: 1–8
  Unlegitimated contacts: Present: 1–4; 9–12
                          Absent: 5–8; 13–16
  Small continuing units of settlement: Present: 1, 2, 5, 6, 9,
                                        10, 13, 14
                                        Absent: 3, 4, 7, 8, 11,
                                        12, 15, 16
  Sovereign kinship groups: Present: Odd numbers
                            Absent: Even numbers
  x: Household is ultimately sovereign group. All cases have
  two or fewer sovereign units, unlegitimated contacts,
  and, of course, a sovereign kinship unit.

TABLE XV

GROUPING OF TABLE XIV'S CATEGORIES BY WEIGHT

Weight	Immanence of Soul		Per Cent Present
	Absent	Present	
4 *	0	1	100
3 *	3	5	63
2	6	13	68
1 **	8	2	20
0 **	6	2	25
Total	23	23	

* Combined for chi-square analysis
** Combined for chi-square analysis

There are five societies which may be considered as affording negative evidence. Two have scores of zero, yet show evidence for a belief in immanence. Three lack such evidence, yet have scores of three. The former are the Iroquois and Orokaiva. The latter are the Nez Percés, Trumai, and Yagua.

The Iroquois are reported to have used exuvial magic and to have practiced cannibalism and scalping. No other society in our sample shows as many evidences of a concept of immanence. At the same time, however, these people had at least six sovereign groups, lived in sizable settlements, and had two sovereign groups organized according to kinship. It is possible that we are wrong in saying that they lacked unlegitimated contacts. The matriarchal pattern extended from the nuclear family to the foundations of the League of the Six Nations, their ultimately sovereign group. This situation may have generated considerable hostility and ambivalence among males. If so, however, there is no strong evidence for it in the reports examined. All things considered, the Iroquois must be taken as an exception to the prediction.

As we noted in discussing monotheism, the Orokaiva may be misclassified. The accounts are not entirely clear about the status of clan and village—whether they are two aspects of one unit or whether they are separate. Apparently the latter possibility is realized on occasion. How often it occurs is uncertain. If the indigenous and traditional pattern is the amalgamation of clan and village into one unit, two consequences would follow. First, the Orokaiva would be considered to have two sovereign units, not three. Second, the feuds among these exogamous clans would be taken as indications of unlegitimated contacts. This would give the Orokaiva a score of two, not zero, and they would cease to provide us with an exception in this chapter. It is clear that more information must be had before these questions can be settled.

The Nez Percés Indians from the plateau along the Snake River in Idaho and Oregon seem to meet many of our criteria for a belief in immanence, yet do not evidence such a notion. In fact, their principal historian, Francis Haines,[3] says that the Nez Percés were unlike many of their neighbors in not taking the scalps of enemies or mutilating their victims' bodies. These people seem to represent a clear violation of our expectations.

By contrast, the Trumai of Brazil's Mato Grosso region may fail our expectation for lack of continuing groups. These people live in a single village. In times past they were numerous, but, as a result of epidemics, they numbered only 43 persons in 1938 and 25 in 1948. Their neighbors treat them with arrogance, and they live in dread of armed aggression and sorcery from alien villages. For these reasons, it is possible that they lack the sense of continuity of social organization required if the individual's powers are to be evidenced and given some extension beyond his own life.

Finally there are the Yagua. These people of northeastern Peru appear, like the Iroquois, to be a real exception to the prediction. A re-examination of the information about them has not unearthed any hints of forces within their society which prevent the appearance of belief in the immanence of the soul.

ALTERNATIVE EXPLANATIONS

One might wonder whether the indicators employed here relate to one or a few of the phenomena of immanence, say exuvial magic and head-hunting, but not to the others, say scalp-taking and cannibalism. This seems not to be the case. The relationship between the category weights and each of these manifestations of immanence is similar, although, partly because no one of them contains a large number of cases, none of these relations is significant.

Only one other social condition of the many reviewed in these chapters proves to be related to a notion of immanence. Societies with important debt relationships are more likely $(p = < .05)$ [4] to possess this belief. This might be indicative of powers which particular individuals have over one another. On the other hand, such an interpretation would imply that debt relationships should be related to reincarnation, and our findings do not sustain that implication. Further, the addition of debt relations to the four indicators employed in this chapter does not make any appreciable difference in their relation to immanence—this despite the fact that none of them is, in turn, significantly and clearly related to the presence of debts.

SUMMARY OF RESULTS

1. Cumulative scores which combine the number of sovereign groups in a society with the presence of unlegitimated contacts, the size of the units of settlement, and the presence of sovereign kinship groups are related positively and

significantly to indicators of a belief in the immanence of the soul.

2. The only other social condition found to be related to a belief in immanence of the soul is the presence of debts. The relationship is positive.

CHAPTER VIII

THE PREVALENCE OF WITCHCRAFT

Witchcraft is one of the dangers that confront most primitive peoples. The individual can never be certain that someone is not turning supernatural forces against him. Even as he sleeps, the spirit of the witch may hover near a man's home waiting to bring death. In some societies, men must hide all the exuviae they produce lest such products be used by a sorcerer against the person from whom they came. The witch may be a man or woman, a member of the society or an alien. He may seek knowledge of black magic for evil uses or he may have such knowledge thrust upon him through inheritance or by the action of spirits. He may harm another in reprisal for some specific injury or to satisfy a heinous greed or merely because it is "in his nature" to do so. In any case, his fellows must guard against him. The problem of this chapter is to explain why some societies experience little witchcraft, perhaps none, and why others are ridden with witches.

There are surprisingly few published explanations of witchcraft or its degree of prevalence. Perhaps the most common proposal mentioned in anthropological reports suggests that black magic is much used only between people who are in close relationship with one another. With one important modification, this seems true of most cases in our sample. The modification forced upon us by the data is that some societies explicitly deny that witches can or will harm their close kin or those who belong to the same ultimately sovereign group as the witch.

But, let us search out other suggestions. Monica Wilson proposes that:

. . . witch beliefs are general in small-scale societies with inadequate control of their environment and dominated by personal relationships, societies in which people think in personal terms and seek personal causes for their misfortunes. . . .[1]

At least a part of this thesis can be tested with our data. We can see if there is a negative relationship between the prevalence of witchcraft and the several indices of social complexity employed in previous chapters. No such relationship appears. Our data also fail to reveal a connection between the prevalence of witchcraft and a society's control of its environment as measured by the abundance of the food supply.

It may also be relevant to inquire whether societies in which the soul is not separated from the body are more likely than others to be ridden with witches. It is possible that such a close linkage of body and soul would imply that people think of one another as personally responsible for their neighbors' misfortunes. The data show such a relationship. Societies that conceive of the soul as immanent are significantly more likely to have moderately or highly prevalent witchcraft ($p = < .01$).

These findings do not properly evaluate Mrs. Wilson's theory, however, for they take no adequate account of her phrase "societies in which people think in personal terms." That phrase would have to be expanded and elaborated before one would know how to collect data appropriate for a test of her hypothesis.

Another explanation of witchcraft's prevalence is found in Kluckhohn's work on the Navaho.[2] While Kluckhohn writes primarily of the Navaho, he occasionally offers a generalization about witchcraft intended for wider application. His essential perspective is that black magic, like any other "cultural form," survives only because it helps the Navaho or their society to survive. Whatever its destructive consequences, Kluckhohn feels that the positive contribution of witchcraft accounts for its existence. What is that contribution for the individual and his society?

For individual Navahos who practice black magic it is:

. . . a means of attaining wealth, gaining women, disposing of enemies and "being mean." In short, witchcraft is a potential avenue to supernatural power. Power seems to be an important central theme in Navaho culture of which gaining wealth, disposing of enemies, and even, to some extent, obtaining possession of women are merely particular examples.

An inadequate memory, lack of the fees for teachers (the teacher of witchcraft needs to be paid only by the sacrifice of a sibling!), or other factors prevent some Navahos from attaining supernatural power through the socially approved route of becoming a singer. For such persons learning witchcraft is a manifest antidote to deprivation. . . . The practice of witchcraft similarly supplies an outlet to those Navaho in whom aggressive impulses are peculiarly strong. . . .[3]

Most Navahos, however, do not practice black magic. What contribution does it make to their ability to live and prosper? Kluckhohn proposes the following advantages for nonpractitioners:

1. It provides a source of excitement, interest, and stimulation.

2. It gives a partial answer to such disturbing experiences as the stubborn persistence of some illnesses or the failure of a curing ceremony.

3. It is a means by which persons of little prestige can get the attention, sympathy, and aid of others.

4. It provides stories and fantasies which are socially validated and which allow the individual to express culturally forbidden interests and desires.

. . . a man can have a daydream involving intercourse with a dead woman without recourse to a witchcraft setting. But he is then likely to have his pleasure dampened by worry over the abnormality of his phantasy.

. . . Whereas, if the phantasy takes the form of repeating (or manufacturing) a witchcraft tale involving this incident or visualizations while listening to another telling such a story, the psychological mechanisms of identification or projection permit the outlet in phantasy without conflict.[4]

5. It allows the expression of direct and displaced antagonisms. It permits "the objectification and alleviation of displaced anxieties arising from the general situation of the Navaho or from the special situation of a particular Navaho at a particular time."[5] In this connection, Kluckhohn stresses the threats which Navahos experience from their scant and uncertain economy, from illness, from stresses within their own society, from the demands of the encroaching white Americans, and from the difficulty of compromising between native culture and the new ways of life which are learned in the American schools. He also suggests that:

. . . Since most hostile impulses must to greater or lesser extent be suppressed, there is need in every society for hate satisfaction. But unless there are some forms of hating which are socially approved and justified, everyone will remain in an intolerable conflict situation, and neuroticism will be endemic in the population.[6]

While nonaggressive responses such as withdrawal, sublimation, or conciliation might be made to a threatening environment, these require special social mechanisms for their promotion and are never fully satisfying means of expressing the hatred which deprivation produces.

To quote again:

. . . It would be too much to say that all societies *must* necessarily have their "witches," i.e., persons whom it is proper to fear and hate and, under defined circumstances, to behave aggressively toward. . . . But no culture which has yet been described leaves "witches" out of its definition of the situation for every sector of life or for every group within the society. "Witches" in this very general sense of "scapegoats" have probably played some part in all social structures . . . Thus the Nazis have had the Jews; the Fascists have their Communists and their "Plutocratic democracies"; "liberals" have the Jesuits (and vice versa). For a period of time the French had the Germans.[7]

6. Witchcraft beliefs make it possible to do something about unpleasant and perplexing experiences. If bad weather is responsible for poor crops, little can be done. If a witch caused the bad weather, the culprit is potentially susceptible to control by the society.

Witchcraft also affords support to the society of the Navaho.

1. It gives dramatic definition to all that is bad, to "all secret and malevolent activities against the health, property and lives of fellow tribesmen." [8]

2. Because the rich or stingy man or the powerful medicine man fears being accused of witchcraft, such potential

accusations tend to prevent "undue accumulation of wealth and . . . too rapid rise in social mobility" and remind all that "capacity for influencing the course of events by supernatural techniques must be used only to accomplish socially desirable ends." [9]

3. "Accusation of witchcraft is . . . a threat which Navaho social organization uses to keep all 'agitators,' all individuals who threaten to disrupt the smooth functioning of the community, in check." [10]

4. Beliefs in black magic also re-enforce the performance of many socially required acts. Thus if the aged are not fed, they may witch against one. Siblings who are ill will be helped lest the suspicion grow that one is trying to arrange their death in order to become a witch. Leaders suspected of having powers of witchcraft are more readily obeyed.

Finally, Kluckhohn notes that witchcraft has been especially prevalent among the Navaho at two periods of their history. The first was at the time of their decisive defeat by the whites and in the succeeding years (1875–1890) when they were creating a new way of life under white supervision. The second came in the 1940's when the United States government forced them to reduce their holdings in sheep in order to preserve the range lands and when there was a sudden upsurge in the number of Navaho who were forced into the general American economic system in order to survive. He proposes that in both of these periods deprivations mounted, and observes that such forms of tension release as alcoholism, the Peyote Cult, and general suspiciousness increased along with witchcraft. These events conform to the general views which we may now summarize.

According to Kluckhohn, witchcraft appears when the following conditions are present simultaneously:

1. Strong deprivations
2. Of unknown or uncertain origin
3. Occurring under social conditions which provide neither nonaggressive means of venting one's tensions and anger nor means which are not socially disruptive
4. In the presence of beliefs supporting the efficacy and availability of magical procedures.

Kluckhohn ends by saying:

. . . my thesis is not that given the amount and kind of aggression which exists in Navaho society witchcraft belief *must* exist. My thesis is only that given these conditions some forms of release must exist. When other forms are inadequate, and when the witchcraft patterns were historically available, witchcraft belief is a highly adjustive way of releasing not only generalized tension but also those tensions specific to Navaho social structure.[11]

While it would be most difficult to evaluate the justice of Kluckhohn's interpretation of witchcraft for the Navaho in particular, we may ask whether it would serve as an account of witchcraft, or of highly prevalent witchcraft, in other societies. Because it contains such a careful synthesis of so many considerations, it merits thoughtful examination.

The Navaho are not the only people in the world who eke out a scanty existence and who know of magical procedures. They also are not unique in facing terrifying or mystifying threats to their existence or in being without socially approved means for expressing their aggressions. Yet, not all peoples facing these problems and knowing of magic become ridden with witches. Within our sample, for instance, the societies of the Copper Eskimo or the Marquesan confront exceedingly difficult problems and forbid the expression of the ensuing tensions, yet lack the pervasive suspicion and fear of sorcery so characteristic of the Navaho. On the other hand, cases such as the Azande, Ganda, Lozi, or Zulu come to mind where sustenance is at least adequate and many means of expressing dissatisfactions and anger seem available, yet witchcraft is endemic.

Let it be clear, again, that none of these points is made to determine the usefulness of Kluckhohn's position as applied to the Navaho. He has presented an interpretation of witchcraft in one society. He explicitly states that he does not view the conditions associated with witchcraft among the Navaho as certain to be necessary or sufficient for producing witchcraft in that society or any other. "My thesis," he says, "is only that given these conditions some forms of release must exist." We, of course, may go further and ask whether the conditions are necessary or sufficient to produce endemic witchcraft. It seems doubtful that, taken together, they are either necessary or sufficient.

Despite these reservations about the widespread applicability of Kluckhohn's theory, it contains important and interesting suggestions from which a more generally applicable explanation of the prevalence of black magic may be derived. These suggestions involve specifying a type of threat or deprivation which is especially likely to be associated with witchcraft. Once this is stated, the fourth of Kluckhohn's four conditions (the presence of beliefs supporting the efficacy and availability of magical procedures) must again be invoked as a necessary condition. The route leading toward an identification of this crucial type of deprivation takes us back to examine a characteristic of witchcraft to which Kluckhohn gives extensive treatment.

THE NATURE OF WITCHCRAFT

The power of a witch does not come from petitions for aid to some deity who may or may not favor his request.[12] Witches have the means to make proto-spirits or mana do their bidding. In witchcraft, the supernatural has no choice but to obey the instructions it receives. A pin thrust into the neck of an image of the witch's victim kills the man outright. The supernatural cannot decide otherwise. If the intended victim does not die, the witch's failure is attributed to someone else's magical skills which were set in motion to protect the victim or to some failure in technical procedure on the part of the witch. There is no hint that the supernatural forces invoked decided not to obey the sorcerer's will because they felt it should not be granted, that his desire was unjustified.

Further, witchcraft is not just another method of aggression, distinguished only by the fact that supernatural means are employed in a mechanical fashion. It is a mode of attack which is, or can be, secret. It is a hidden poison, not hand to hand combat. Victims may employ another magician to locate the attacker and such means as oracles or ordeals may aid in ferreting out the offender, but these are, at best, uncertain. Moreover, to harm another person through black magic implies that the sorcerer's cause would not receive public support. If his desires would be sanctioned by his fellows, he might use one of many other means to achieve his ends—the legitimate feud, the public trial, the open attack. If he could not deliver the blow himself, his kin or community or the spirits would help him in a just cause. When magic is employed, however, the cause need not bear public scrutiny.

Thus, the very nature of witchcraft as a social relationship suggests that it is a way of handling deprivations of a special kind. That people are faced with an ungenerous and capricious climate does not imply that they will attack one another. Nor are such interpersonal hostilities to be expected when, in a harsh country, the society to which men belong provides no satisfactory ways of meeting adversity. In Kluckhohn's own words, it may be then that "neuroticism will be endemic in the population."

But witchcraft, with its objective of harming some individual or group, implies that the reason underlying its use is hatred of others—others whose purposes toward one are close, important, persistent, and uncontrolled by legitimizing social arrangements.

The widespread use of black magic suggests a serious lack of legitimate means of social control and moral bonds. It implies that people need to control one another in a situation where such control is not provided by means which have public approval. One thinks, then, of the intimate but unlegitimated situations described in the preceding chapter.[13] We shall expect endemic witchcraft when those situations are present.

We shall consider witchcraft to be prevalent whenever the ethnographer reports that it is believed to be the source of all or much of the illness or misfortune which a people encounter or a frequent cause of death. We shall consider it of little consequence when the observer says explicitly that it is absent or of very minor importance. All other cases will be rated as intermediate between these extremes.

FINDINGS

Table XVI presents the result of applying this approach. It shows a strong relationship between the prevalence of witchcraft and the presence of important but unlegitimated relations among people. The level of significance at which this relationship holds is beyond .0005.

TABLE XVI

PREVALENCE OF WITCHCRAFT AND PRESENCE OF UNLEGITIMATED
OR UNCONTROLLED RELATIONSHIPS

Prevalence of Witchcraft	Unlegitimated or Uncontrolled Relationships		
	None	Within the Society *	With Other Societies *
High	1	7	10
Intermediate	14	2	5
Low	9	0	1
Total	24	9	16
Per cent high	4	78	62
Per cent intermediate or low	96	22	38

* Combined for chi-square analysis

Further inspection of the table indicates that there is no substantial difference in the association of each of the two types of unlegitimated situations described in Chapter VII with the prevalence of black magic. In addition, the table indicates that the greatest difference in the frequency of such unlegitimated relationships occurs when the highly prevalent row is compared with the low and intermediate rows.

NEGATIVE EVIDENCE

There are two societies which clearly do not meet our expectations. The Tanalan is witch-ridden in the absence of the unlegitimated relations we have described. The Yahgan has such relations, but is reported to have little or no witchcraft. Both are examined in the paragraphs below.

It is possible that the Tanala were misclassified when they were said to have endemic witchcraft. It is true that they attribute many of life's misfortunes to the action of sorcerers, but some mishaps are blamed on fate. In addition, these people believe that most cases of illness are caused by ghosts. There is no indication of intimate relations among members of different ultimately sovereign groups. Neither the kinship organization nor any other is reported as generating great strains within the society.

The problem of defining the boundaries to ultimate sovereignty may exist for the Yahgan. The nuclear family's household appears to be the ultimately sovereign unit. These families are bound together by intermarriage and co-operative ceremonies. We have taken these conditions to be productive of highly prevalent black magic. However, as we observed in discussing monotheism among these people, it is possible that the neighborhoods of such families are organized more clearly and frequently than we first supposed. There are, for example, reports that a man who could get the support of powerful kin in his neighborhood could become an informal leader of consequence. We also learn that a man's paternal kin were bound to give him aid if he asked for it. Finally, the observers tell us that each kin neighborhood had its own name and its members considered themselves as having a common territory. The case is, therefore, ambiguous, but may involve misclassification.

In summary, one cannot say that either of these negative instances provides a firm refutation of our scheme. Each of them may have been misclassified.

ALTERNATIVE EXPLANATIONS

As we have already seen, the explanations of witchcraft in terms of intimacy of contact, or in terms of the formulations of Wilson and Kluckhohn, require elaboration and modification if they are to be applied in a prediction of the prevalence of witchcraft. Each supplies some important ingredient for our final interpretation and prediction.

In addition to these three earlier approaches, we may ask whether the presence of endemic witchcraft is significantly related to any of the social conditions employed in earlier chapters for other predictions. The answer is negative.

NOTE ON TWO CASES OF WITCHCRAFT IN WESTERN SOCIETIES

It is interesting to speculate on two cases of prevalent witchcraft in Western societies. The first is the frequently mentioned rise of black magic at the close of the Middle Ages and the beginning of the Renaissance. The second is the classic American case of the witch scare in Salem, Massachusetts.

Both seem to have elements of the kind stated in our theory as productive of endemic witchcraft.

Lowie reminds us that:

. . . Not in the so-called Dark Ages, but in the centuries following "the revival of learning" the belief in black magic gained ascendancy to a point never known before or since and led to the death of thousands of victims, not through the ebullition of popular wrath but by the solemn machinery of duly constituted legal authority. . . .[14]

Perhaps the significance of this period of the Renaissance and the Enlightenment—roughly from 1500 to 1750—is that it coincided with a dramatic change in the political structure of western Europe. Small local and regional units were giving way to national states. For at least two centuries the very allegiance of populations and the legitimacy of their governments were in flux. In addition, the commercial revolution and a host of other changes were helping to stimulate the rise of a new social stratum, the middle class, and were promoting the growth of Protestantism and other heresies from Roman Catholicism. Thus, the two types of situation we have associated with a high prevalence of black magic were present in a society in which there were strong beliefs both in magic and in association with evil supernaturals for personal gain. A superficial examination of the case seems to indicate that witchcraft should have increased in frequency according to our theory.

The situation in Salem, Massachusetts, has been given a searching examination in recent years, and it, too, appears to fulfill our criteria.[15] Historical accounts show that the government of the Colony of Massachusetts had drifted into chaos. Under Cromwell, the Colony was almost autonomous.

A Puritan theocracy governed. Charles II curbed this theocracy by appointing a royal governor in 1683. When Charles was deposed in 1689, William of Orange removed Governor Andros, but devised no new form of colonial government until 1691. The new charter proved unpopular and the regime it established was unstable. These upheavals in colonial administration were accompanied in Massachusetts by much internal dissension over the proper roles of church and state, bitter controversies concerning Puritan doctrine, and disrupting Indian wars.

The village of Salem (now a part of Danvers) shared in the general confusion which had, in 1692, the year of the witchcraft hysteria, left Massachusetts without an English governor and weakened the colony's once effective theocracy. Salem, unlike most of Massachusetts, also suffered from a breakdown of judicial practices. The local judges simply ignored the dispassionate and orderly procedures commonly employed for examining accused witches and abandoned the ordinary rules of evidence. It appears that these extraordinary circumstances allowed the situation to develop from the accusation of a single person to the accusation of hundreds and the execution of twenty. Once again, it seems that the absence of legitimate political procedures in a society where black magic was considered possible generated widespread fear of witches.

SUMMARY OF RESULTS

1. Witchcraft tends to be prevalent when people must interact with one another on important matters in the absence of legitimated social controls and arrangements.[16]

2. Among the societies in our sample, such close and important but unlegitimated contacts fall into two categories: those between ultimately sovereign groups and those within such groups. Each of the categories is related in about the same degree to the prevalence of witchcraft.[17]

3. Further, we can determine whether inadequate control of the environment as judged by the nature of the staple food or the abundance of the food supply is related to the frequency with which evil sorcery is experienced. These measures of environmental control are not related to the prevalence of witchcraft in our data.

CHAPTER IX

THE SUPERNATURAL AND MORALITY

For Jews and Christians, God is the source and mainstay of human morality. The Ten Commandments and the Beatitudes are crystallizations of His pervasive interest in moral behavior. And, as the Biblical history unfolds, we find the idea emerging that God, too, is a moral being. Abraham stands before God and forces Him to admit that a city with only one good inhabitant should be spared the divine wrath lest one innocent man be harmed. God is delighted when Job proves that he loves God for Himself, not for the blessings He may bestow. The Son of God makes love of one's neighbor as important as love of God, and, as God incarnate, suffers and dies to deliver men from immorality and unfaithfulness.

The people of modern Western nations are so steeped in these beliefs which bind religion and morality, that they find it hard to conceive of societies which separate the two. Yet most anthropologists see such a separation as prevailing in primitive societies. In this chapter, we shall search for a clarification of the relation of the supernatural and morality and for the conditions under which supernatural sanctions provide explicit support for human moral relations.

We may begin with the classic statement by Edward Tylor [1] that most primitive peoples see no connection between supernature and morality. (For Tylor, religion was

a "belief in Spiritual Beings." He does not seem to have defined ethics or morals.)

Tylor cited the following points to support his generalization:

1). The deities of primitives do not seem to be interested,
or are not interested in most cases, in the conduct of individuals toward one another. They are concerned only that
people perform the appropriate religious rituals.

2). There frequently is no connection between what a
man does on earth and the kind of existence he has in the
afterlife.

3). Some primitives treat their gods lightly—scolding
them, cheating or deceiving them in rituals or sacrifices, and
trying to force them to act as men wish.

Evidence for Tylor's position fills a large part of Wilson D.
Wallis' review of *Religion in Primitive Society*.[2] In the same
vein, Reo Fortune closes his study of the highly ethical
religion of the Manus by saying:

. . . Tylor is entirely correct in stating that in most primitive
regions of the world religion and morality "maintain themselves
independently." Primitive religion generally enjoins, as the
correct means of setting man right with the supernatural, ritualistic acts such as sacrifice, libation, the proper rites over the
dead, and the keeping of a variety of taboos and more or less
aesthetic ceremonials. The Manus religion stands out against
this background in clear and bold relief. It is a concentration on
setting man right with man as the way of setting man right with
the supernatural. . . .[3]

The anthropological voice which disputes these conclusions most strongly is Malinowski's. He wrote:

. . . From the study of past religions, primitive and developed,
we shall gain the conviction that religion has its specific part to

play in every human culture; that this is fundamentally connected with faith in Providence, in immortality, and in the moral sense of the world; and that this faith in turn demands a technique for its expression, a technique which offers possibilities of communion and prayer, of revelation and miracle; finally, that every religion implies some reward of virtue and the punishment of sin. . . .[4]

Or, again:

. . . Myth, ritual, and ethics are definitely but three facets of the same essential fact: a deep conviction about the existence of a spiritual reality which man attempts to control, and by which in turn man is controlled. . . .[5]

What shall we make of such divergent opinions? Perhaps a review of some evidence and the clarification of some words will help.

First of all there is no doubt that societies exist which fulfill some or all of Tylor's three types of evidence for the absence of a relationship between the supernatural and morality. But there likewise is no doubt that other primitive groups meet none of these criteria. We can be certain that Tylor's view is not universally valid for primitive societies, but that it does fit some of them.

We also find[6] that all societies possess rules governing moral relations and ethical concerns. Linton even proposes that a large number of these rules are substantially the same in all societies.

This brings us to the meaning of the words morality and ethics. We have already defined mana, spirit, magic, and religion and provided some evidence of the empirical utility of those definitions. What do Tylor and Malinowski mean when they speak of morals and ethics? Clarity about this matter is a prerequisite for evaluating their positions.

Neither Tylor nor Malinowski provides us with a definition. We can, however, get some sense of what they mean from examining their use of these terms.

In common speech, morals and ethics refer to rules or standards governing behavior in particular kinds of situations. The key to their popular meaning lies in a description of those situations.

We speak of moral relationships only when the participants are self-conscious beings, usually human or supernatural. One does not refer to moral relations among atoms or mice or trees. Further, not all relations among self-conscious beings are moral. We usually require that certain additional conditions be met. We ask that these beings facilitate the achievement of one another's goals. We require that this facilitation be given intentionally and without coercion. We demand that it be accepted intentionally and without coercion. If any of these conditions are unfulfilled, common usage does not consider the relationship truly moral. Morals are social rules which specify the behaviors required of those who enter moral relationships and seek to maintain them.

Consider some examples which do not fulfill all of these criteria. We do not usually think of the newborn infant as immoral when he discommodes his parents by getting them up in the middle of the night or refuses to drink the milk which they lovingly offer him. We say that, while they have facilitated his goals with intention and without undue coercion, he has not so accepted their efforts—indeed he is incapable of such acceptance until he is older. Likewise we do not think a man immoral if he has gifts or attentions forced on him or if he refuses demands from those to whom he is not obligated.

To summarize, a moral relationship exists to the extent that self-conscious beings intentionally and freely facilitate the achievement of one another's goals and intentionally and freely accept this facilitation from each other. Unless all of these conditions are met, the relationship is not regarded as moral in character.

The word "ethical" connotes the rules or relationships which exist when *individuals* have moral relations with each other. An examination of Tylor's writing suggests that this is what he has in mind.

By contrast, one may think of moral relations between a group and one of its members. Patriotism, the filing of an honest income tax return, and other expressions of a member's feelings of obligation and loyalty to a group fall under this heading. No English word seems especially fitted for referring to this variety of moral relationship.

Malinowski's thinking about moral relations has more of this latter meaning as its referent. He says, "You cannot worship in common without a common bond of mutual trust and assistance, that is, of charity and love," [7] and he continues:

The essentially sound methodological principle is that worship always happens in common because it touches common concerns of the community. And here . . . enters the ethical element intrinsically inherent in all religious activities. They always require efforts, discipline, and submission on the part of the individual for the good of the community. Taboos, vigils, religious exercises are essentially moral, not merely because they express submission of man to spiritual powers, but also because they are a sacrifice of man's personal comfort for the common weal. But there is another ethical aspect which, as we shall see, makes all religions moral in their very essence. Every cult is associated with a definite congregation; ancestor-worship is primarily based on the family; at times even on a wider group, the clan; at times it becomes tribal, when the ancestor spirit is that of a chief. The members of such a group of worshippers have natural duties towards each other. The sense of common responsibility, of reciprocal charity and goodwill, flows from the same fundamental idea and sentiment which moves clansmen, brothers, or tribesmen to common worship. . . .[8]

It seems clear that Tylor and Malinowski have different situations in mind when the former notes the relative absence of connections between morality and religion among primitives while the latter declares that they are joined together in all cases. Tylor has in mind the absence of situations in which supernatural actions are thought to follow the fulfillment or infringement of obligations generated by the moral relationships which exist between particular individuals. Malinowski refers to the moral relationships which must exist among members of a group before those members can engage in common worship or before members of the group will be willing to "sacrifice . . . personal comfort for the common weal" in keeping taboos, vigils, and religious exercises.

We may note that failure to fulfill taboos and other ritual obligations brings supernatural punishment to individuals and groups, and that one or more taboos are associated with all known religious systems. Further, there is at least one universal taboo—the one forbidding incest—which is plausibly understood as designed to preserve the moral relations within the family and which seems to be punished supernaturally in a great many primitive societies.

Recalling our conceptions of the nature of mana and spirits, we can also appreciate that these forms of the supernatural must be linked intimately to the support of moral relations. It would be strange indeed if the deities which represent sovereign groups were totally indifferent to actions which violate the bonds of loyalty that bind members to those groups. One would also be surprised if the mana which stands for potentialities of objects did not sometimes harm men who infuse those potentialities with antisocial purposes. Among such potentialities may be those which uphold the importance of social solidarity and which imply that men who infringe the conditions of that solidarity are evil.

To summarize our thinking, the ethnographic evidence supports the judgment that moral relations between particular individuals are not always subjected to supernatural sanctions. It also makes plausible the conclusion that such sanctions apply to one or more moral relationships among group members in all religious systems. Those sanctions may be supplied by spirits or by the activation of mana. Finally, we conclude that the presence of supernatural sanctions for some immorality is implied by our conceptions about the nature of mana and spirit. Thus, in some respects, the supernatural is frequently involved in supporting human morality.

THE SUPERNATURAL AND INTERPERSONAL MORALITY

But what of the fact that supernatural control is exercised over the moral relations between particular individuals in some societies and not others? Three hypotheses come to mind which might explain this finding:

1). Any important but unstable moral relationship between individuals, whether as particular persons or as members of some group, will evoke supernatural sanctions to buttress their fragile association.

2). Supernatural controls cannot be exercised over inter-personal relations unless the number of persons having inter-ests peculiar to themselves has become great enough to create a large number of social relations in which people interact as particular individuals, rather than as members of some group.

3). Supernatural controls are exercised over interpersonal relations in all societies, but this belief becomes explicit only when the conditions cited under the first hypothesis force people to become aware of the facts.

The first hypothesis suggests that we shall find super-natural sanctions applied whenever it is necessary to reinforce unstable but important moral relations between individuals. One rationale for this would declare that when such relations are unstable they threaten the constitutional arrangements of the group involved and the symbolic representation of those arrangements—the appropriate spirit—will be invoked to remind participants of their fundamental ties to one another.

The second hypothesis says that people will not con-ceive of themselves as subjected to rules governing inter-personal moral relations unless such relations exist among them in a relatively clear form. This would imply that we should look for sanctions—including supernatural sanctions —governing relations among individuals only in cases where such relations exist.

The third hypothesis proposes that actions of mana and spirits may govern interpersonal moral associations in all societies, but become explicit only in some societies. We might assume, in support of this hypothesis, that people make explicit and verbal only what they must. Research on language shows that it is fruitful to consider words as a series of tools by which people guide and manipulate their own behavior and that of others. Words stand for things other than themselves. They represent those aspects of the universe to which men attend. Further, men pay particular attention to those features of their world which they find especially important and, at the same time, difficult and problematic. By this line of reasoning, when desired interpersonal relations become difficult to achieve or maintain, beliefs about those relations including their connection with the supernatural must become explicit.

It can be seen that the third hypothesis is only a variant of the first. Unlike the first, however, it suggests that supernatural sanctions may attach to interpersonal relations in all of the simpler societies.

METHODS OF STUDY

Our data do not permit us to make clean distinctions in testing these three hypotheses. The very indicators of interpersonal differentiation required by the second hypothesis are also likely to be among the sources of malintegration and strain required for Hypotheses One and Three. Further, we have not been able to find clear evidence for the kind of universal supernatural undergirding of interpersonal moral relations specified in Hypothesis Three, and cannot, therefore, distinguish between it and Hypothesis One. We can, however, examine the association of supernatural sanctions and various indicators of interpersonal specialization or strained relations in societies. The following were thought of as especially likely indicators which should be positively related to supernatural sanctions: debt relations, social classes, individually owned property, specialties in noncommunal activities, close but unlegitimated relations, primogeniture, and the existence of a matri-family.

Take the case of debt relations as an example. When one man loans another something of value on the strength, at least in part, of the borrower's personal willingness to make repayment by a particular time, there exists a situation fraught with special perils. The lender will recognize that there is always some danger of not being repaid. The borrower appreciates the lender's fears. He also is likely to feel somewhat inferior to his creditor, and resentful that this should be their relationship. Between lender's suspicions and borrower's resentment, the relationship may become tense. Growing estrangement is always possible.

Such divisive forces also threaten the peace and stability of organizations to which both debtor and creditor belong. The purposes and potentialities of those organizations (as embodied in spirits and mana) may modify potentially disruptive relations by providing supernatural sanctions for honesty, for charitableness, and for faithfulness in meeting obligations. Thus supernature may become active because forces which make for differences and potential conflicts among members of an organization also threaten that organization's life.

No detailed explanation is needed to show that social classes, individually owned property, specialized, but noncommunal activities, or unlegitimated interdependence may be classified with debt relations as potential sources of interpersonal differences or discord and distrust. We should, however, comment on some indicators not previously employed in these chapters: the practice of primogeniture and the structure of a matri-family.

Primogeniture means that the oldest child, usually the oldest male, is the sole heir of his parents' property. Although the lot of the other children may be ameliorated by such devices as requiring the oldest brother to care for his siblings, primogeniture is widely recognized as productive of jealousy and dislike.

Finally, there is the case of the matri-family. In some societies, the mother or her relatives have authority over the husband and over children. It is rare, however, that women, rather than men, perform those tasks which are economically most significant. As a consequence, one might expect that husbands would resent the disparity between their authority and their economic importance.

A related situation, which we have tabulated under the heading "matri-family," occurs when, in polyandry, several men are married to the same wife. Four of our 50 societies have this practice. Not only are there likely to be strains flowing from competition for the wife's favors, but the several husbands are likely to face difficult problems of competing authority in making family decisions or in rearing the children.

In relating these several indicators to supernatural sanctions we must recognize that the information we have been able to record is inadequate on several counts. Perhaps its most persistent deficiency is the absence of direct evidence that particular relationships between people meet our criteria of morality or that the persons concerned are interacting as particular individuals rather than as members of a group. All one can say is that the records contain those instances in which sanctions of supernatural origin are applied to persons because these persons help or harm other members of the same society. Let us see what this will include and what will not be tabulated.

We shall include:

a). All cases in which the supernatural forces initiate the sanction, as, for example, when spirits help the deserving or when mana harms a man whose purposes in relation to other persons are repugnant to the nature of mana.

b). Cases in which magical techniques in human hands punish offenders or support good men, providing that people believe magic was given to them by spirits for the express purpose of aiding the good and punishing the evil.

The following are not included:

c). Cases in which magical techniques are used by people to help or harm others without the presence of a legitimating myth saying that the spirits gave magic to man for the promotion of good and the suppression of evil.

d). Cases in which behavior is subjected to supernatural sanctions without explicit reference to the rationale that the sanctions were imposed because the behavior helped or harmed other people. For example, most incest taboos state merely that sexual relations with certain persons are supernaturally forbidden. They do not say that such relations are forbidden because of the harm which they bring to participants. Or, to take another instance, we may find a belief that a priest who stumbles over the words of a chant will fall ill. Again, if there is no corollary belief that he becomes sick because of the harm his error in speech brings to his people, this instance will not be tabulated.

e). Cases in which the persons concerned do not belong

to the same ultimately sovereign group. The application of black magic to alien enemies would be an example.

As criteria a) through e) specify, we shall tabulate those instances in which, as members of the same society, we may assume that participants have some minimal moral commitments to one another. Within that framework, we count cases in which supernatural sanctions apply to certain behaviors because people are assisted or deprived by those behaviors. It is probable that all beliefs in supernatural sanctions have this criterion of behavior's effects on other people as their implicit rationale, but we confine our count to those cases in which this rationale is explicit. Thus we tabulate those instances in which participants should understand that the consequences of their behavior for other persons or for groups of people evoke a supernatural response. This is as close as we were able to come in relating supernature to the support of morality.

The ethnographers report several types of consequences which spirits or mana apply to behavior. It is convenient to group these under three headings:

1). Effects on health (e.g., good health, cures for sickness, illness, death, malformed offspring).

2). Effects on experiences in the afterlife (e.g., special pleasures or tortures including cases in which actions of the living affect the comforts which the dead receive). (It is assumed that the morality of the deceased when he was alive determines the way his descendants treat his soul after he dies.)

3). Other effects on the living (e.g., accidents, misfortunes, or mishaps other than those specified under effects on health).

FINDINGS

Table XVII shows the relationship between each of our several possible sources of specialization or tension, and the presence of supernatural sanctions of the kind previously described. It also relates those sanctions to other possible indicators which seemed less promising than the ones discussed earlier in this chapter.

TABLE XVII

SELECTED SOCIAL CONDITIONS AND SUPERNATURAL SANCTIONS

Social Conditions	Supernatural Sanctions		p
	Absent	Present	less than
Association Predicted *			
Debts: considerable	1	19	+.01
Debts: moderate or none	8	11	
Noncommunal specialties: 3 or more **	4	14	+.35
Noncommunal specialties: 2 or less	10	20	
Social classes present	2	25	+.0005
Social classes absent	12	8	
Individuals own important property	4	23	+.05
Individuals do not own important property	8	11	
Primogeniture present	1	12	+.05
Primogeniture absent	13	21	
Matri-family present	6	9	−.30
Matri-family absent	6	25	
Unlegitimated contacts present	11	15	−.10
Unlegitimated contacts absent	3	19	

Social Conditions	Supernatural Sanctions		p less than
	Absent	Present	
Others ***			
Communal specialties: 5 or more	6	15	****
Communal specialties: 4 or less	8	18	
Sustenance: grain crops	2	18	.05
Sustenance: other than grain crops	12	16	
Sovereign groups: 4 or more	3	9	
Sovereign groups: 3	4	10	.95
Sovereign groups: 2 or less	7	15	
Communal groups: 1 or more	8	23	.50
Communal groups: none	8	11	
Unorganized social categories: 1 or more	5	21	
Unorganized social categories: none	9	13	.20
Total population 400 or more	2	16	.10
Total population 399 or less	12	17	
Settled in villages, towns or cities	8	21	****
Not settled in villages, towns or cities	6	13	

* Probabilities given for one tail of the distribution if finding is in the expected direction. Findings in the expected direction are preceded by a plus (+) sign. Findings in the contrary direction are preceded by a minus (−) sign.

** I.e., more than age and sex.

*** Probabilities are given for both tails of the distribution.

**** Probability is more than .99.

Of the seven indicators that we anticipated would have a significantly positive association with supernatural sanctions, four fit our expectations: the presence of considerable debt relations, social classes, individually owned property, and primogeniture. One other, the number of noncommunal specialties, is in the expected direction, but not significant. The two remaining indicators are negatively, though not significantly, associated with sanctions from spirit and mana. These indicators are the presence of unlegitimated contacts and matri-families.

We find, then, a cluster of three indicators related to interpersonal differences in wealth which have a positive and significant association with supernatural sanctions. Perhaps primogeniture, with its provision for the inheritance of substantial property by only one child in a family, should also be considered to represent an indication of differences in wealth.

It is interesting to note that societies with more than one of the indicators in this cluster of four almost always evidence supernatural sanctions associated with interpersonal relations. Table XVIII provides the relevant information. We

TABLE XVIII

NUMBER OF INDICATORS OF DIFFERENCES IN WEALTH AND SUPERNATURAL SANCTIONS

Supernatural Sanctions	Number of Indicators				
	0	1	2	3	4
Present	2	4	7	11	4
Absent	4	4	0	1	0
Total	6	8	7	12	4
Per cent present	33	50	100	92	100

may also observe that only nine (or 24 per cent) of the 37 societies for which pertinent data are available lack such sanctions. This indicates that these sanctions are widespread in our sample.

Table XVII contains further information of interest. It shows significant, but unpredicted, relations between supernatural sanctions and the presence of grain crops as a primary source of sustenance. We also find that there is a positive relationship of almost significant magnitude between supernatural sanctions and population size. Both of these indicators reflect increasing specialization. Both are usually interpreted as referring to increasing wealth in a society.

From these results it seems that indices of specialization, especially those linked to differences in wealth among a society's members, are likely to be related to the presence of supernatural sanctions for interpersonal relations. None of the associations is perfect, but there are enough of them to suggest that our hypotheses lead us to a consistent pattern of relevant conditions.

We can also propose explanations for the two cases in which relationships appear in a direction contrary to our expectation—those with unlegitimated contacts and matrifamilies. Beginning with the first, we may recall that unlegitimated contacts are classified as involving members of the same society or, as in some cases of intermarriage, as concerned with persons from other societies. It seems reasonable that relations with persons from other societies have less of a moral quality than those with one's fellow countrymen. With aliens, one has no tradition of mutual co-operation and mutual enhancement. In addition, if spirits symbolize the constitutional arrangements of human groups, we are not likely to find that such arrangements, and, hence, the spirits, influence persons alien to these groups. Either of these hypotheses leads to the prediction that supernatural sanctions in support of interpersonal morality are less likely to govern unlegitimated relations between members of different societies.

The data in Table XIX show a tendency consistent with this prediction. When we combine the figures for societies that lack unlegitimated relations with the information from societies in which unlegitimated contacts occur among members of the same society, and compare this sum with data from societies in which unlegitimated relations with aliens occur, we find a difference which is in the predicted direction and which is significant beyond the .01 level of probability.[9]

TABLE XIX
UNLEGITIMATED CONTACTS AND SUPERNATURAL SANCTIONS

| Supernatural Sanctions | Unlegitimated Contacts | | |
	Absent *	Within a Society *	With Aliens
Present	20	7	8
Absent	2	2	9
Total	22	9	17
Per cent present	91	78	47

* Combined for chi-square analysis

We can extend this line of reasoning in considering the case of matri-families. We expected that such families would be the source of strain between husbands and their wives' relatives. This, we said, might generate the need for supernatural sanctions which would help to support the unstable family relationship. Suppose, however, we reverse this expectation after the manner of the preceding paragraph. Suppose we assume that unstable families are less able to produce such sanctions simply because their members are less likely to have a moral relationship with one another. Suppose, further, we combine this prediction with the one just made for unlegitimated relations with aliens. We would then expect that societies in which such unlegitimated relations existed or in which matri-families were the norm would be less likely than others to have supernatural forces acting in support of interpersonal moral contacts. The data of Table XX conform to this expectation. The expected difference occurs at a level of probability beyond .02.[10]

TABLE XX

MATRI-FAMILIES, UNLEGITIMATED CONTACTS, AND SUPERNATURAL SANCTIONS

Supernatural Sanctions	Matri-Family					
	Absent			Present #		
	1 * ʼ	2 * ʼ	3 * #	1 *	2 *	3 *
Present	14	4	7	5	0	4
Absent	0	1	5	3	1	2
Total	14	5	12	8	1	6
Per cent present	100	80	58	63	0	67

* 1—Unlegitimated contacts absent
* 2—Unlegitimated contacts within a society
* 3—Unlegitimated contacts with aliens
ʼ, #—Combined for chi-square analysis

These last two findings are of considerable importance for our understanding. They imply that, for the production of supernatural sanctions, it is not enough to have stress and strain in required relations among individuals. If those relations are not moral and fully legitimate, the foundations for such sanctions are less likely to be present. This conclusion indicates that research on morality and the supernatural must first establish that a moral relation exists in the population studied.

ALTERNATIVE EXPLANATIONS

Apart from the theories of Tylor and Malinowski, little has been written about the conditions which evoke supernatural sanctions for moral acts. As we have seen, Wallis [11] simply restates and documents Tylor's position that "In most pre-literate cultures religion has few ethical implications." Schneider [12] proposes that spirits known on the Island of Yap, like the Yap people themselves, need not punish incest as soon as it occurs because incest does not rend the society's lineage structure. He does not, however, suggest why the spirits punish incest at all. There are innumerable other descriptions of supernatural sanctions, many of which are of great interest and promise to be important in future thinking about the topic, but none of which provides a solution to our problem.[13]

An important exception appears in Julia Brown's study of deviations from the sexual mores.[14] She drew a sample of 110 societies from the Human Relations Area Files and, among other things, investigated the problem of the types of sexual offenses which were punished by supernatural forces. She finds that certain behaviors [15] are punished by supernatural agents in all societies where these particular acts are considered to be offenses. By contrast, other sex-related offenses are less likely to be subject to supernatural punishment.

This result suggests that the nature of the misconduct

partially determines whether supernatural sanctions will be invoked. She observes in connection with offenses which are always punished supernaturally:

. . . These tabus seek mainly to restrict marital relations. It may be that the punishment for their infringement is left to supernatural agents for the simple reason that violations are difficult to detect. A second reason for the absence of social sanctions may be that the injured and the injurer belong to the same family group, and members of the larger society for that reason lack interest in exacting penalties. Unrelated individuals may consider it unfortunate that the deviators are injuring themselves and their kin, but refuse to stop or punish the acts. A third possible reason for the predominance of supernatural sanctions is that unborn or infant children are frequently the ones thought to be hurt by the offenses. Since such youngsters lack human protectors other than the very parents who are injuring them, society nominates supernatural agents to serve as surrogate parents and additional protectors. . . .[16]

Brown's research indicates that future studies of morality and the supernatural should take the type of offense concerned into account before making predictions. It would be well, however, to note certain differences between her work and the approach taken in this chapter. Brown does not tell us what she means by "supernatural agents." This may mean mana or spirits. What is more important, she has not restricted supernatural sanctions to those situations in which an individual is punished for behaviors which harm other individuals. In that sense her definition of the task is broader than ours. On the other hand, it is narrower in that, unlike the present research, she does not tabulate instances in which rewards as well as punishments are given for interpersonal conduct.

Finally it should be noted that a majority of the societies

in Brown's sample do not consider most of the sexual acts she lists to be misconduct. This implies that future studies must do more than take the nature of the offense into account in their predictions. To make those predictions maximally precise, some attempt must be made to forecast the kinds of societies in which a given act will be considered evil.

Brown's work provides us with a most important lead for future studies of morality and the supernatural. It also indicates that such work will be highly complicated, involving a whole series of interrelated predictions.[17]

SUMMARY OF RESULTS

1. Contrary to Tylor's formulation, a considerable proportion of the simpler peoples do make a connection between supernatural sanctions and moral behavior.

2. Supernatural sanctions for interpersonal relations are most likely to appear in societies in which there are interpersonal differences according to wealth.

3. Societies with matri-families or unlegitimated contacts with aliens are less likely to possess such sanctions.

CHAPTER X

CONCLUSION

Chapter by chapter we have searched in nature for the origin of beliefs concerning supernature. Chapter by chapter we have made some progress in that search. But, what bearing do our findings have on the broad, speculative conceptions with which we began—conceptions of mana, spirit, and supernature itself? What, in general, have we learned from applying our conceptions to particular theological beliefs? We must now face questions such as these.

IMPLICATIONS FOR THE CONCEPTIONS OF THE SUPERNATURAL

Only a few of the notions sketched in Chapter I have been brought into direct contact with data. The idea employed over and over in succeeding chapters is that the belief in a particular kind of spirit springs from experiences with a type of persisting sovereign group whose area of jurisdiction corresponds to that attributed to the spirit. This guiding premise led to the isolation of the sovereign groups associated with beliefs in high gods, ancestral spirits, and reincarnated souls. In an elaborated form it led us to a pattern of social conditions associated with the belief that souls are immanent in bodies and to another pattern of social conditions associated with polytheism.

Our study of the prevalence of witchcraft was shaped in

part by the assumption that magic represents the infusing of mana with human purpose. This assumption is among those developed in the first chapter's presentation of the nature of the supernatural. Finally, in the study of the supernatural and morality, we employed our assumptions about spirit and mana to predict the conditions under which supernature would punish immorality in human affairs.

There is, however, a finding which may cast doubt on the identification of spirits with sovereign groups. This concerns the soul's immanence and it deserves comment.

The material on immanence seems to contradict our theory of spirits. It shows that one kind of spirit, the individual's soul, is more likely to be conceived as coessential with a man's body if that man is relatively free of involvements in sovereign groups.

It might be argued, of course, that this is not an exception to our theory. One might say that the notion of immanence tends to reduce the soul from a spirit to something like mana. Mana, our account states, can exist without being attached to sovereign groups. Unfortunately, no satisfactory method for submitting this interpretation to an empirical test has yet come to mind.

IMPLICATIONS FOR ALTERNATIVE THEORIES

In the first chapter, we considered several explanations of supernature. These accounts were alternatives to the explanation which guided our investigations. Some of them could be discarded at once as illogical or contrary to fact. Others seemed of doubtful value.

Our findings about primitive religious beliefs make possible some further evaluation of four of these alternative theories.

1. Beliefs in supernature are fantasies which arise to compensate for deprivations.

Our findings suggest additional reasons for doubting the accuracy of this view. The material on high gods and ancestral spirits, for example, indicates that the extent to which these deities are active in human affairs is a function of the presence of organized groups which embody certain purposes. There is no relation between the degree of help to be expected from these spirits and such a measure of deprivation as lack of food. On the other hand, we find a certain realism, instead of compensatory fantasy, in the positive relation between intimate but unlegitimated contacts and a belief in the prevalence of black magic.[1]

Should one take as support for a compensatory theory of religion the discovery that supernatural punishments for immorality occur where individuals differ in wealth? Probably not. The data in Chapter IX do not support any simple compensatory scheme. They indicate that supernatural sanctions for moral conduct are likely to appear only when the relations among men are moral and fully legitimate.

Perhaps the following would be a statement consistent with our knowledge: Deprivations, as such, do not seem to explain the appearance of an idea of supernature or a particular kind of spirit or the extent and nature of that spirit's participation in worldly events. Instead, it seems that such ideas are founded on man's experience with purposes embodied in the structure of social organizations. Once a conception of supernature comes into being, individuals or groups may put it to some compensatory use.[2] Special studies are required to determine the conditions under which people will develop compensatory notions and will, additionally, employ religious conceptions, instead of other ideas, to make up for the difficulties men encounter.

2. Conceptions of many types of spirits, especially of superior gods, spring from man's acquaintance with such great natural forces as the winds or sun or sea.

At least in the case of superior gods, we can say that this account is unsatisfactory. Many peoples who witness a spectacular change of the seasons replete with typhoons, long droughts, and torrential rains have no beliefs in superior gods. By contrast, there is a relation between the number of specialized occupations in a society and the likelihood that its members believe in such deities.

3. Gods, especially monotheistic gods, are projections from men's experiences with their fathers.

This theory now seems implausible on two grounds additional to those cited in Chapter I. The scheme would imply that a belief in high gods should be as prevalent as the presence of fathers. Our data contradict that implication. Second, we find that high gods are active in human affairs only if communal groups are present in a society and that high gods, if active, often show little concern for the morality of human relations. By contrast, human fathers always take an interest in the world, are active in it, and usually have strong moral concerns.

4. Spirits represent the element of chance in human experience—they symbolize and rationalize the unknown, irrational, and mysterious.

Contrary to this theory, our information shows that spirits are associated with the presence of organized decision-making groups or purposes clearly identified with particular individuals. This is not to say that spirits are completely understood or completely rational. Our evidence does, however, associate the presence of many spirits with order and purpose, not chance and chaos.[3]

To summarize: Where our findings provide additional evidence, that evidence is contrary to these alternative explanations of supernature. The same evidence is consistent with the interpretations advanced in these chapters.

FUTURE STUDIES OF RELIGIOUS ORIGINS

After so many years of fruitless debate about problems like the origin of language, the state, or religion, it is natural that scientists are highly skeptical about theories concerned with these topics. Such theories are commonly discarded as soon as they appear on the grounds that it is impossible to prove what they assert. This treatment is usually a case of making the right decision for the wrong reason. Many explanations of social origins deserve to be forgotten, but not because they cannot be demonstrated to be true.

As we saw in Chapter I, all assertions about causation are equally unprovable in an ultimate and absolute sense. Many are improvable through increasingly sophisticated investigation.

When we study the sources of beliefs concerning supernatural events, we can, as in the present investigation, require that the causes we advance escape the known limitations of alternative explanations. We can demand that those causes be found in association with the effects we believe they produce. We can ask that the causes we believe are at work appear in a variety of settings in which their effects are found. In all these respects, our present findings support explanations advanced in these pages.

To strengthen our confidence in the account given here for a belief in spirits, we may continue to search for cases in which changes in sovereign groups and in religious beliefs have occurred. We can determine whether the former routinely precede the latter as our theory predicts. We may also apply successive refinements to our observations and to the factors we hold constant in our work. We can, in addition, study with profit those situations in which people come to disbelieve in supernatural forces.

To summarize, these comments about studies of causation do not imply that the present research on theology is definitive. They do indicate that explanations of religious beliefs should not be discarded as inherently unprovable— with the tacit assumption that the causes of other phenomena can sometimes be demonstrated as beyond doubt.

INTERPRETATIONS OF PRIMITIVE BELIEFS

Some social scientists who can agree that we may fruitfully study the problem of religion's origin, will have a different reservation about our studies. They will be troubled by the thought that natives in these 50 societies may not conceive of mana and spirits in the same fashion as such ideas are described in our theories. The importance of this reservation also deserves review.

At many points we insisted that the conceptions of supernature employed in these pages were somewhat speculative. One can document the presence of beliefs in gods who created all reality. One does not say, however, that monotheists think that these spirits, as suggested in our analytic scheme, provide unity in the world's diversity. Similarly, we have presented a description of mana which seems in keeping with anthropological findings, but we must not assert that any medicine man would assent to our account of mana's nature.

We may claim that many of our conceptions lead to verified predictions. If they err or are "right for the wrong reasons" this can be discovered. If primitives would disagree with our conception of their notions, it is even possible that we, not they, are the more accurate. In any event, subsequent research can decide such issues.

Misinterpretations of religious beliefs may, of course, be a source of the errors in our predictions. Whether because of flaws in our theoretical scheme, in the data, or in the application of theory to empirical observations, we always find some societies which do not meet our expectations. An effort has been made to identify such societies in order to bring future research to bear directly on these critical cases.

UNEXPLOITED EXPLANATIONS

And what of the many notions in Chapter I that are not employed directly in our predictions? What place do they have in our work?

Any general conception of the origin of spirits or witchcraft or ethical religion must be consistent with equally general conceptions of supernature itself and mana. The discussion of all these matters in Chapter I was important for later predictions precisely because it suggested that ideas which we did use to make those predictions were plausibly consistent with conceptions which would embrace additional features of the supernatural. Without some such assurance of consistency with closely related explanations, it would be hazardous indeed to venture so far with a theoretical scheme.

INTERRELATIONS AMONG THE PREDICTORS

As part of this evaluation of our work, we also may ask whether the indicators devised to predict each particular supernatural phenomenon are related significantly to that phenomenon alone. If, for example, unlegitimated contacts were strongly associated with monotheism, we should wonder whether an alternative account of high gods had been uncovered. Table XXI shows relationships between these indicators and beliefs other than the one for which they were employed in prediction.

The ten predictors are related at the .10 level of probability or beyond to seven beliefs. This is not appreciably different from the number of such relationships which should occur purely by chance were all these beliefs independent of one another and were the predictors similarly independent.

Of more importance for an evaluation of our findings is a detailed examination of the data presented in this table. Consider, for example, the positive relation shown in Table XXI between the number of noncommunal specialties and the presence of high gods. We saw in Chapter III that the number of sovereign groups continues to be related to the presence of high gods when the number of noncommunal specialties is controlled. We also found that the relation of noncommunal specialties to the presence of high gods disappears when the number of sovereign groups is held constant. Therefore, the number of noncommunal specialties is not an alternative explanation of beliefs in high gods.

TABLE XXI
INTERRELATIONS AMONG PREDICTORS AND BELIEFS *

Predictor	Belief	Two-Tailed Probability
Number of sovereign groups	**	**
Number of noncommunal specialties	Monotheism	+.10
Number of sovereign kinship groups	**	**
Pattern of conditions to predict reincarnation	**	**
Pattern of conditions to predict immanence of soul	Monotheism	−.01
	Prevalent witchcraft	+.10
Unlegitimated contacts	Moral supernatural	−.10
Primogeniture	**	**
Individually owned property	**	**
Social classes	Superior gods	+.05
Debt relations	Active ancestrals	−.10
	Immanence of soul	+.10

* The plus (+) sign before some probabilities indicates that the relationship is positive; the minus (−) sign indicates that the relationship is negative.

** The predictor is not related at the .10 level or beyond to any belief other than the one which it was originally designed to forecast.

Because the predictors for monotheism and prevalent witchcraft are part of the pattern of conditions devised to forecast immanence of soul, they cannot be controlled out of that pattern in Table XXI. Their presence explains why that pattern has some notable relationship to monotheism and prevalent witchcraft. At the same time, however, neither of these indicators, by itself, is significantly related to immanence of soul.

In Chapter IV, we found a relationship between the presence of social classes and the number of superior gods. It reappears in Table XXI. As we discovered in Chapter IV, our sample of societies must be enlarged before the meaning of this association can be explored. The reasons are described in more detail in Chapter IV.

We have already discussed the relations shown in Table XXI between a moral supernatural and unlegitimated contacts. This material appears in Chapter IX.

Finally, Table XXI reports some almost significant associations between debt relations, on the one hand, and both the activity of ancestral spirits and the soul's immanence on the other. Do these associations modify our earlier explanations? We may begin with the connection between debts and active ancestrals.

Table XXII shows that the addition of debt relations to our predictors of the activity of ancestral spirits provides some interesting interactions. Both the absence of debt relations and the presence of sovereign kin groups contribute to the likelihood of a belief in active ancestral spirits. Debt relations may stand for an impersonality among individuals which is deleterious to the cohesion of kinship groups and, hence, to the continued influence of the ancestral dead.

Table XXIII indicates an interaction between the total immanence score and debt relations in predicting a belief in the immanence of the soul. In each grouping by immanence score, a belief in immanence becomes more likely if debt relations are present. Once again, we may propose that the impersonality and the interpersonal differences in

TABLE XXII

DEBT RELATIONS, SOVEREIGN KINSHIP GROUPS, AND
ACTIVE ANCESTRAL SPIRITS

Active Ancestral Spirits	Debt Relations Absent Sovereign Kinship Groups *		Debt Relations Present Sovereign Kinship Groups *	
	Absent	Present	Absent	Present
Present	5	9	1	8
Absent	2	0	4	3
Total	7	9	5	11
Per cent present	71	100	20	73

* Excluding nuclear families

TABLE XXIII

DEBT RELATIONS, IMMANENCE SCORES, AND
IMMANENCE OF SOUL

Immanence of Soul	Debt Relations Absent			Debt Relations Present		
	0,1 *	2 *	3,4 *	0,1 *	2 *	3,4 *
Present	1	4	1	2	7	5
Absent	7	2	2	5	1	0
Total	8	6	3	7	8	5
Per cent present	13	47	33	28	88	100

* Immanence scores

status implied by debt relations could be responsible for
the trend. In this case, such conditions would identify a
man's powers with his person and, hence, increase the likelihood of a belief that his spirit was immanent in his body.
This possibility and the interactions in Table XXII should
be explored further in a larger sample of societies.

In conclusion, there are some interactions among the
social conditions from which we have predicted theological

beliefs. At the same time, we have no strong evidence that associations found in Table XXI require great modifications of our earlier explanations of those beliefs. A more elaborate exploration of possible interactions among our predictors awaits the availability of a larger sample of societies.

INTERRELATIONS AMONG THE BELIEFS

Another matter of interest in evaluating our results concerns the presence of patterns among the beliefs under study. Is witchcraft likely to appear in societies which believe in the soul's immanence? Do polytheism and beliefs in active ancestral spirits go together? Table XXIV provides the answer.

Only three significant relationships appear out of the 20 that are possible. This is not appreciably more than the num-

TABLE XXIV

INTERRELATIONS AMONG SUPERNATURAL BELIEFS *

Beliefs	1	2	3	4	5	6	7
1. High god					−.10		
2. Superior gods						−.10	+.02
3. Active ancestrals							+.05
4. Reincarnation							
5. Immanence of soul						−.01	+.10
6. Prevalent witchcraft							
7. Supernatural sanctions for morality							

* The values in the table are the two-tail probabilities obtained from chi-square tests. All probabilities reaching .10 or beyond are recorded. A minus (−) sign before a probability indicates a negative relationship between the variables. A plus (+) sign indicates a positive relationship.

ber of significant associations which might be obtained purely by chance.

We find that the presence of polytheistic deities is associated with the presence of supernatural sanctions for morality. This is probably a function of the common association of these two beliefs with the degree of specialization and differentiation in a society. We also find that such supernatural sanctions are likely to appear in societies with active ancestral spirits. This may be due to the fact that one way of coding ancestrals as active is by their punishment of human immorality or their rewarding of good behavior. Finally, we see that societies espousing the soul's immanence are likely to have prevalent witchcraft. The reason for this association is obscure, although witchcraft may be facilitated and encouraged by such a belief. We do know, however, that the social conditions related to prevalent witchcraft are not significantly associated with immanence of soul and that the converse is also true.

In general, then, it is possible to find any pair of the beliefs we have studied present in the same society. This relative independence among the beliefs corresponds to our finding that the conditions from which each is predicted are usually independent of those which relate to the others. One must remember, of course, that this degree of independence may not exist in some particular societies. We find, for example, that beliefs in witchcraft came under heavy and increasingly successful attacks in the societies professing Christian, Judaic, or Mohammedan monotheism. It may be that, beyond a certain point, there is a gross incompatibility between a highly developed monotheism and beliefs in witchcraft. This would, for example, be a reasonable derivation from the notion that, as the governance of mana by powerful spirits increases, the use of mana for human magic must be increasingly restricted. This is a testable hypothesis. Presumably there are many other incompatibilities which can appear among the beliefs reviewed in these chapters if the social conditions are appropriate. In this regard, it might be especially instructive to study the successes and failures of missionaries who try to implant new beliefs in a variety of divergent cultures. One might then ask such questions as: Under what conditions can Christianity be adopted without interfering with conceptions of ancestral spirits or black magic and under what conditions is the importation of Christian monotheism accompanied by the destruction of native beliefs about the supernatural?

DISBELIEF IN THE SUPERNATURAL

In another vein, we may ask what our notions of the supernatural imply for the appearance of disbelief in mana or spirits. Any satisfactory explanation should account for disbelief as well as faith.

Given our ideas about the experiences to which spirit and mana correspond, we should expect any of the following conditions to produce disbelief:

a). Lack of contact with the primordial or constitutional structures of a society.

b). Alienation from those structures.

c). The assumption that all, or the most significant, features of those structures are knowable and controllable by human effort.

Isolation and alienation from a society's primordial and

constitutional structures prevent one from having experiences from which beliefs in the supernatural can arise or gain support. To assume that humans can know and control all, or the most important, aspects of such structures, is to destroy, in principle, many of the features which give certain social organizations a supernatural aura—their properties of invisibility, immortality, pervasiveness, unknownness, inescapability, and their control over conduct through what seems to be the direct induction of purpose.

To illustrate and evaluate these implications and to suggest conditions which commonly produce this kind of isolation, alienation, or assumption would require far more space than is appropriate here. However, these implications seem consistent with what little is known about the generation of disbelief, they have much in common with the accounts of other social scientists concerning the origin of disbelief,[4] and they appear to be testable proposals. Finally, they indicate that our notions of experiences which produce beliefs in the supernatural may also allow us to account for disbelief.

THE PLACE OF THE THEORY IN THE STUDY OF SOCIAL ORGANIZATION

A most important reason for undertaking studies such as these is to help fill one of the great gaps in our understanding of man and society. We have known for a long time that ideas about the supernatural were intimately related to the maintenance of motivation in the individual and integration in society, to the ultimate evaluations which men make of their experiences and the most fundamental bonds which unite them to each other. Despite the host of distinguished studies devoted to the varieties of human worship and belief, the object that provoked all the panoply of religion and magic remained elusive. We have had, from the standpoint of natural science, only Durkheim's pregnant suggestion of an answer. The main objective of this research has been so to modify and elaborate Durkheim's approach, as to make it susceptible to empirical verification.

Once some progress is made in that direction, other things become possible. We begin to see in the connection between sovereign groups and spirits a direct empirical link connecting the independent decision-making structures in a society—the structures by which goals are chosen and rewards and responsibilities allocated—and the supernatural. Philip Rieff observes:

Men became religious when they had to approach and rationalize the chaos of powers by which they were moved and their destinies sealed. But from Hobbes to Weber there has been an insistent, ironic voice saying that religious man is really, at bottom, political man. All theologies are metaphors of politics. . . .[5]

From our data, it has been possible to explore in direct and concrete terms the bonds and interactions of political matters, broadly conceived, with magic and religion.

Again, once we have some clearer picture of what mana and spirit represent—of the objectives of magic and the objects of worship—we may begin to take a fresh look at the procedures employed in magic and religion; to understand more fully why particular doctrines and practices are especially appropriate to particular times and places in history. This may enable us to go beyond saying that religion contains such aspects as faith, worship, penitence, forgiveness, moral implications, and the rest. Perhaps, knowing the source of encounters with spirits, we can begin to say *why* religion contains such features, and *why* some features are more evident than others in particular societies.

Perhaps some of the ideas presented here will also prove useful in understanding the operation of organizations other than societies. Although one rarely talks in supernatural terms when describing large-scale organizations, small, persisting groups, communities, or crowds, they seem to contain many phenomena homologous with those discussed here. We do speak of the "spirit" of such groups, of their "character" and "competence," [6] of their atmosphere, of the hold which they have on their members, of the deep involvement which people develop in connection with such organizations, and of the "sacred" quality of their relationships. Primordial and constitutional structures are features of all human association.[7] Something of sovereignty is also a pervasive aspect of social life. These considerations may help us to approach once more such archaic phenomena as "the collective unconscious" and "the spirit of the folk" and bring them within our scientific understanding.

Many of these matters lend themselves to study in the laboratory. It is especially likely that there, under controlled conditions, one can separate out the constitutional and primordial aspects of social relations, modify the forms they take, and pursue their consequences.

Our findings reaffirm the persistent sociological judgment that participants in a society experience and formulate significant aspects of that society's total structure, that participants are not limited to experiencing and formulating only those aspects of their society with which they, personally, are in intimate touch. If there is any value in the idea of a group mind, it lies in its stress on the notion that the overarching structure of social organizations acts upon the participants in those groups, shaping their conduct and giving some ultimate meaning to the roles which individuals play. Our work encourages one to take seriously notions of this order.

Finally, these studies offer support for certain testable propositions about social organization:

1. Under certain conditions, participants in groups perceive those organizations as having a life of their own—as containing a persistent "corporate personality" which is somewhat independent of, and different from, the lives of the individual members and which acts on the world in a predictable fashion.

2. Sovereign groups, that is, groups which exercise original, independent, and legitimate jurisdiction over some area of social relations are more likely to be perceived as having such a corporate personality than are nonsovereign groups, particular social roles, or such social categories as age or sex which often are not organized as groups.

3. The purposes of particular human individuals are likely to be seen as peculiarly theirs when those purposes are not also present in the corporate personalities of sovereign groups to which those individuals belong. Our data concerning the soul's immanence is especially pertinent to this proposition.

4. A corporate personality can be active in human affairs if its organizational arrangements provide persisting links between its purposes and the lives of individuals. This proposition is exemplified in certain of our findings: High gods are active when a society possesses several communal groups; the ancestral dead are active in earthly events when a society has sovereign kin groups; individuals renew their corporal

existence when their personalities continue to have impacts on small, sovereign residential units.

5. One of a corporate personality's purposes may be experienced as separate from the others, and as active in the world, if this purpose is embodied in a specialized occupation. This principle seems consistent with our findings about the superior gods.

6. The nature of a sovereign group's unity determines the nature of the special roles that will be appropriate embodiments of particular purposes of that group. (See the discussion of the fitness of communal and noncommunal roles, respectively, for embodying the purposes of kin and nonkin societies.)

7. If the purposes of a sovereign group are frustrated by persons regarded as participants in that group's moral order, the group's corporate personality is seen as having power to reform the offenders. (See the discussion of supernatural sanctions for morality in legitimated social relations.)

8. If the purposes of a sovereign group are frustrated by persons regarded as alien to the group's moral order, the group's corporate personality is not seen as having power to *reform* the offenders.

9. If these offenders are members of another society, the corporate personality of one's own society may be invoked to *immobilize* or *destroy* them.

10. If these offenders are participants in one's society but alien to its moral order (e.g., wives who were reared in a different society), sanctions other than those of the group's corporate personality will be employed to immobilize the offenders or nullify the effects of their activities. (See the discussion of witchcraft.)

APPENDIX I

(A. Content to be Recorded; B. Code; C. Classification of the Sampled Societies; D. Table XXV.)

A. Content to be Recorded

The attached list of content to be recorded should be used as a guide rather than a mechanical enumeration of categories. There is no need to report materials in the order presented. Instead, it will be easier to record information as it appears in the monographs consulted. At the same time, it will be helpful if the content-numbers are recorded in the left margin of a running account opposite appropriate observations.

The attached list is not exhaustive. We are looking for the scope, nature, and strength of integration in the societies studied. We also look for signs that the integration of these societies or the suborganizations within them is subject to strain. We need to assess the pervasiveness and seriousness of those strains. We need to be clear about the location of those strains and the consequences they have. We need to be sensitive to conditions or devices which reduce the negative consequences of what might, in other circumstances, be more important strains. Evidence along all of these lines should be recorded even if it does not seem to fall within the categories of the attached list.

1. *History:* Length of occupancy of present territory, duration of present culture patterns, relations with other peoples in the near and distant past, migrations.
2. *Site:* Features of climate, soil, terrain, waterways, transportation routes which notably limit or determine the relations of this group with other groups or the kind of culture found in this society.
3. *Population:* Estimates of past and present size. Any demographic peculiarities. Any feelings about having children. Distribution of population over terrain by density and type of unit.

4. *Sustenance:* Principal and subsidiary means of production. Surplus of wealth produced? Personnel involved in production by social characteristics and by interdependencies involved in their work. Stability of standard of living through the year and across the years. Level of technology employed. Principal vegetable and animal food (include fish). Source of the knowledge people have about sustenance methods. Methods of exchange.

5. *Kinship:* Principal personnel and their interdependencies. Authority, residence, descent, and inheritance patterns.

6. *Allocation:* Of the values produced in the society (wealth, respect, honor, protection, prestige, health, affection, etc.), who gets what, when, and how? Rules of inheritance. Private property. Personal profit. Bases of inequality of reward. Degree of inequality of reward. Stability of inequality of reward.

7. *Differentiation:* (In addition to points noted above.) What is the nature and degree of specialization developed in sustenance activities, war, relations with other societies, kinship, education, religion, etc. Remember that widespread skills represent limiting, but not negative, cases of specialization.

8. *Moral Integration:* Collective ceremonies—e.g., initiation, planting, burial, harvest, curing, etc. Who participates and what effects are believed by participants to be produced? Evidence of altruistic acts. Evidence of acts of devotion to other individuals or to group. Evidence of recurrent hostility sublimated (e.g., joking) or overt. Evidence of disputes and tensions because of individual differences in goal or outlook. Evidence of individual or subgroup mobility or of the desire for such mobility (whether vertical or horizontal mobility and in relation to religion, kin, etc., as well as to economic relations). Nature and frequency of crime or other negative deviance (e.g., suicide, divorce, nonsupport, mental disorder and illness. Include accidents to person and property.) Frequency, methods, degree of fear, and personnel, connected with witchcraft, sorcery, black magic. Punishments invoked for deviance by adults or children. Interpretation of causes of deviance as given by participants.

9. *Political Organization:* Nature and size of largest political

unit and important subsidiary units. Problems of integrating activities within and between units. Nature of participation in their activities. Methods of decision-making. Personnel involved and method for selecting same. Tenure. Topics of decisions made and nature and effectiveness of sanctions employed to enforce conformity. Organization for relations with other societies including trade and war. Frequency of such intersocietal relations.

10. *Religion and Magic*: Principal classes of supernatural entities, their relations to one another, to man in general, and to particular men. Are they believed to be restricted in this society in their relations to men? What are their motives? How may men relate to them? Is there an afterlife? What is it like and for whom? Do men have careers in the afterlife? Are special personnel involved in relating to supernaturals? How are they selected, what do they do, and in what ways are they rewarded or restricted? How may the typical member of the society relate to supernaturals? What are the principal techniques of magic? Is it used often for antisocial ends? How are supernatural powers obtained by men?

B. Code

All of the items in the code which follows are defined and discussed in appropriate chapters throughout the text. The chapters in which these presentations appear are designated in parentheses after the Arabic number specifying the column in which the data are recorded in part C of this Appendix.

Unless otherwise specified, a Code of Y means "Uncertain" and a Code of X means "Uncodable."

Col. 1: (II) *Principal Source of Food:*
Record what the ethnographer reports to be the staple food or foods consumed. If root crops and products of animal husbandry are co-staples or if grain crops and animal husbandry provide co-staples, record by crop only.
0. Collecting, gathering
1. Fishing

2. Herding—nomadic
3. Herding—settled
4. Agriculture—root crops
5. Agriculture—grain crops
6. Hunting
7. Hunting or fishing and root crops
8. Hunting or fishing and grain crops
9. Harvesting from trees which require some care if they are to bear a crop

Col. 2: (II) *Amount of Food Produced:*

Take into account the quantity of food produced in relation to the needs of the population. Where possible, depend on explicit statements by the ethnographer rather than on personal estimates.

0. Famine not uncommon.
1. Low—amount a matter of some uncertainty, requiring constant effort to obtain enough to meet minimal requirements.
2. Adequate—there is a general expectation that the amount produced will exceed bare subsistence needs.
3. Plenty—surpluses of food are readily obtainable.

Col. 3: (II) *Degree of Threat from Armed Attacks by Alien Societies:*

This estimate is a function of three considerations: a) the likelihood of such attacks, b) the likelihood of their being successful, and c) the damage suffered from such attacks. More explicitly, societies vary in the probability that they will suffer armed attack from the outside, and in the ease with which they seem able to repulse such attacks. Damage suffered from attack also varies. For example, armed attacks may be only glancing raids, performed to "blood" warriors. At the other extreme are large campaigns resulting in many casualties, extensive property damage, and subjugation by a conquering invader. Take into account only attacks by other people who lack guns and other Western military technology.

  0. Little or no likelihood of such attacks, or such attacks are easily warded off.

  1. Some, but not certain, likelihood of such attacks and the success of warding them off is somewhat uncertain.

  2. Considerable—attacks are certain to occur and it is likely that they cannot be warded off successfully, or attacks may occur with uncertain success, but there is also possibility of large casualties, extensive property damage, or subjugation by an invader.

  X. Uncodable.

Col. 4: (II) *Size of Population:*

Refers to the population of the ultimately sovereign organization. Sometimes this is available from an ethnographer's estimates or from official census reports. In other cases, it may be inferred.

a) The total population of several ultimately sovereign organizations may be divided by the number of such organizations to obtain an average.

b) Populations may be known to fall within the largest of the size categories listed below, although their exact size is not known.

c) Populations may be known to fall within the smallest of the size categories listed below although their exact size is not known.

d) If the number of dwelling units occupied by nuclear families in the ultimately sovereign organization is known, it may be multiplied by five for a population estimate.

  0. 1–49

  1. 50–399

  2. 400–9,999

3. 10,000 or more

Col. 5: (II) *Unit of Settlement:*

Refers to the local communities in which most of the population is settled.

0. Population is settled in households, hamlets, or scattered rural neighborhods. There are no villages, towns, or cities.

1. Population is settled in villages or encampments, each with at least 50 people, and/or there is a kraal, compound, village, or encampment specially designated as that of a chief or king. There are no towns or cities.

2. Population, or part of it, is settled in one or more towns (a local community of 300 or more people). There are no cities.

3. Population, or part of it, is settled in one or more cities (local communities having 2,000 or more people).

Col. 6: (II) *Individually Owned Property:*

An individual owns property if he has the legitimate right to determine the way the property shall be employed, or to determine the distribution of benefits realized from the property, or to dispose of the property or some part of it. His rights in these respects need not be held by him exclusively, but he should have larger powers of determination concerning the property than other persons who share ownership in that property. Individual rights to property do not exist, however, when some person (such as a headman or elder) is given wealth with the tacit or explicit understanding that it is his to distribute to the population according to customary criteria. In this classification, property refers to anything which is important in the production of the society's more significant means of sustenance. Such means of sustenance include sources of food which are important, though not among

the staples. Property important in the production of such means of sustenance may take
many forms. Among them are land, tools,
domestic animals, seed, or magical techniques
employed to ensure success in production.

o. Individuals do not own economically significant property.

1. Individuals own property which is used in
producing what the ethnographer designates
as forms of sustenance, but not those which
he calls the most important forms of wealth
or the staple foods.

2. Individuals *can* own property employed in
producing what the ethnographer designates as the most important forms of wealth
or the staple foods.

Col. 7: (II) *Debts:*

Classification records the presence and size of
loans which individuals or groups are obliged
to repay. The loans may consist of goods or
services. It excludes loans when the obligations for repayment are determined by rules
of kinship or such ritual relations as blood
brotherhood. The intent of this exclusion is to
eliminate the less formal and contractual kinds
of borrowing which frequently occur and
which, presumably, do not reflect the degree
of impersonality and specialization of relationship related to other kinds of debts.

o. None—the ethnographer denies that such
debt relations exist or fails to mention
them.

1. Moderate—some debt relations exist, but
there is no indication that they are frequent
or that they are of a size that debtors find
difficult to repay.

2. Considerable—debt relations exist and the
ethnographer mentions that some debtors
find it difficult to repay the loan.

Appendix I: Classifications and Supplementary Tables

Col. 8: (II) *Amount of the Bride Price:*
Refers to size of payments, if any, required to obtain a wife.

0. None—ethnographer explicitly reports that no price is charged or mentions none.
1. Moderate—price exists, but does not involve more than six months of labor on behalf of the bride's family or does not change the standard of living of the groom's family or its members.
2. Considerable—price charged exceeds the specifications listed under category 1.

Col. 9: (II) *Social Classes:*
Refers to the existence of differences in wealth among individuals or families in the population. Such differences do not include situations in which some leading figure, such as a chief, receives wealth which he then is expected to redistribute to his people, his own standard of living not being greater than that of others. Apart from these cases, however, a code of "present" does not require that greater wealth remain in a man's hands all of his life, that he be able to transmit it to some heir of his choice, or that differences in wealth be productive of social privileges.

0. Social classes absent
1. Social classes present

Col. 10: (II) *Specialties in Noncommunal Activities:*
Code records the number of such specialties up to 3 or more.
These are behaviors which meet the criteria presented below and are not listed under Col. 11.

a) They are not performed by all persons in the society nor by all persons holding a particular age or sex role or a given role in the nuclear family.
b) They are directed primarily toward meeting

the needs of one or more individuals, as
such, rather than the needs of sovereign or
nonsovereign organizations.

c) They involve the production of some object or
service (or repair of an object) for the use
of some healthy adult member of the unit
studied, other than the maker or repairer,
when the maker or repairer is recognized
by the adult served as providing such a
special service.

Col. 11: (II) *Specialties in Communal Activities:*
Code gives number of such specialties up to 9
or more.

These are behaviors which conform to the
following stipulations:

a) They are performed only by persons who
meet some customary criteria of competence (ascribed or achieved).

b) Those criteria are not obtained through normal socialization for an age or sex role or a
role in the nuclear family.

c) The behaviors concerned are directed primarily toward meeting the needs of some
sovereign or nonsovereign organization
rather than the needs of particular individuals as such.

Such specialties will almost always include
any political offices, magical or religious roles,
many educational and socializing roles, and
slaves.

Col. 12: (II) *Sovereign Organization:*
Code gives number of such organizations up
to 9 or more.

These organizations have original and independent jurisdiction over some sphere of social life. An organization has original jurisdiction if only that organization can legitimately originate a decision in some sphere
of social life. It has independent jurisdiction

if no other organization and no individual can
legitimately abrogate its decisions.

a) The group or its representatives must meet at
least once a year.

b) It must have customary procedures for making
decisions, such as rules for taking a vote or
sounding out opinions; acknowledged roles,
whether formal or informal, which participants hold in decision-making (e.g., representative, officer, voter, audience, nonofficial participant, member, constituent, consultant).

c) The group must be considered legitimate by
its members. This means that the members
must approve of the group's existence, its
goals, and its procedure of operation. They
may or may not agree with all aspects of
the group's organization, but there must
not be evidence that they challenge the
desirability or justice of its existence or its
general purposes and procedures.

d) There must not be evidence which suggests
that the group is perceived by its members
as failing to persist into the indefinite future.

e) The group must have three or more members.

f) It must make decisions on actions which have
a significant effect on its members (e.g.,
war and peace, the punishment of crimes,
the distribution of food, the allocation of
the more important means for producing
sustenance, the formation of alliances with
other groups, the allocation of "civic" duties such as taxes, conscription for military
or labor service).

g) It must not be an agency of another organization. This usually eliminates such organizations as armed services, magical and
religious organizations, groups of slaves,

specialized divisions of a government, specialized divisions of an economy such as the organization that operates a market or cultivates crops or tends the herds, and educational or socializing organizations such as schools and organized age-sets.

h) It must be viewed as a distinctive organization by its members over whom it has jurisdiction.

Further:

i) The nuclear family—that is, any group consisting of the partners to a marriage and the children of their union—will always be called a sovereign organization unless there is clear evidence that its members have little or no attachment to each other. A polygamous family is counted as a single nuclear family.

j) The local community will always be called a sovereign organization unless there is clear evidence that it lacks some property specified in a) through h) above.

k) Organizations will be counted as meeting criterion a) above, if there is an effective obligation among participants to join together for common and customary action under stated circumstances (such as common defense or the sharing of food in time of disaster).

l) When a group seems to meet the foregoing criteria but there is some conflicting evidence, the case will be coded as uncertain.

Col. 13: (III) *Nature of Third Sovereign Organization— Territorial:*

0. Household, hamlet, scattered rural neighborhood, small nomadic band—see Col. 5, Code 0.

1. Village—see Col. 5, Code 1.

2. District, sector—any political organization

which unifies two or more units coded as 0
or 1 above and which is not codable as 3,
4, or 5.

3. Town, city—see Col. 5, Codes 2 and 3.
4. Chiefdom—any political organization with a
chief executive which unifies two or more
units coded as 0, 1, or 3 above.
5. Kingdom—any political organization with a
chief executive which unifies two or more
chiefdoms.

Intertribal League—any political organization
which unites two or more tribes but is not
codable as a kingdom. For a definition of
tribe see Col. 14, Code 7.

9. No third unit.
X. No purely territorial organization (i.e., not
having a territorial locus).
Y. No data.

Col. 14: (III) *Nature of Third Sovereign Organization—
Kinship:*

0. Household—the nuclear family.
1. Extended family—two or more nuclear families united by consanguineal bonds such as
those between parent and child or between
two siblings.
2. Lineage—a consanguineal kin group produced by a rule of unilinear descent when
it includes only persons who can actually
trace their common relationship through a
specific series of remembered genealogical
links in the prevailing line of descent.
3. Gens—a patrilineal sib. A sib is a consanguineal kin group acknowledging a traditional bond of common descent but unable
always to trace the actual genealogical connections between individuals.
4. Kindred—a bilateral kin group of near kinsmen who participate together in important
ceremonial occasions involving relatives

and who are expected to support one another against outsiders. It is never the same for any two persons except siblings.

5. Clan—meets three specifications: a) it is based explicitly on a unilinear rule of descent which unites its central core members, b) it has residential unity, and c) it exhibits actual social integration—i.e., positive group sentiment and a recognition of in-marrying spouses as an integral part of the membership.

6. Phratry—two or more sibs who recognize a purely conventional unilinear bond of kinship.

7. Tribe or kin-based union of tribes—a political union of two or more sibs, clans, phratries, or moieties,* (or a political union of two or more extended families which is not otherwise classifiable in this column) providing that each of the groups in question is exogamous within itself and endogamous within the union, and providing that representatives of these exogamous kinship groups comprise the government of their union.

8. Uncertain.

9. No third unit.

X. Not a kinship organization.

Y. No data.

Col. 15: (II, III) *Nature of Ultimately Sovereign Organization —Territorial:*
See code categories for Col. 13 above.

Col. 16: (II, III) *Nature of Ultimately Sovereign Organization —Kinship:*
See code categories for Col. 14 above.

Col. 17: (III) *Nonsovereign Organizations:*
Code records the number of such organizations up to 9 or more.

* A moiety is one of a dichotomous pair of sibs or phratries.

These are groups which meet criteria a, b, c, d, e, h, and k for sovereign organizations, but which do not meet one or more of the following criteria for sovereign groups: f, g, or the stipulation that the group's jurisdiction shall be original and independent.

Col. 18: (III) *Nonsovereign Communal Organizations:*
Code records the number of such organizations up to 6 or more.

A communal organization provides goods, services, or decisions for members of a sovereign group from which it gets its powers and responsibilities. The following groups will always be counted as falling within the meaning of this definition if they are not sovereign groups:

1. Agencies of government: courts, legislatures, executive bodies.
2. Religious organizations whether of laymen or of special functionaries.
3. Organizations devoted to curing or magic.
4. Standing armed forces, police, officer cadres.
5. Organizations devoted to social welfare activities: e.g., helping the poor or stricken.
6. Educational organizations.

Col. 19: (II, V) *Sovereign Kinship Organizations Other than the Nuclear Household or the Ultimately Sovereign Group:*
Code gives number of such organizations up to 9 or more.
An exhaustive list of organizations categorized in this column appears in Codes 1 through 7 of Col. 14.

Col. 20: (II, V) *Ultimately Sovereign Group Organized on Kinship Principle:* (see Col. 14, above, for a list of groups organized on this principle).

0. No
1. Yes

Col. 21: (V) *Unorganized Kinship Aggregations:*

Code gives number of such aggregations up to 9 or more.

Refers to kinship classifications given in Col. 14 above, when these are not organized as groups, that is, when they lack the characteristics listed in Col. 12 (sovereign organizations) or Col. 17 (nonsovereign organizations).

Col. 22: (X) *Matri-Family:*

Refers to the presence of one or more of the following features as characteristics of the kinship arrangements: matri-locality, matri-lineality, or the normative expectation that husbands are subordinate in power within the family to their wives or to certain of their wives' relatives.

0. Absent
1. Present
2. Present as polyandry or adelphogamy

Col. 23: (X) *Primogeniture:*

Refers to cases in which, in all families in a society, the oldest child, usually the oldest male, is the sole heir of his parents' property. Primogeniture is coded as present even when this inheritance pattern obligates the heir to care for his siblings; the eldest child inherits the property of his uncles or aunts instead of his parents; the head of a kin unit larger than the nuclear family is the sole heir of all property belonging to that unit.

0. Absent
1. Present

Col. 24: (VII) *Unlegitimated Contacts:*

Refers to social relations having *all* the following characteristics:

a) People must interact closely with one another for the achievement of common ends. In this sense, they are intimate.

b) These relations were not developed with the

consent, tacit or explicit, of all concerned, or

c) These relations are not such that persons with conflicting objectives and desires can resolve their differences through commonly agreed upon means such as courts or community councils.

The following will always be counted as fulfilling these requirements:

a) People are required to obtain (or frequently do obtain) a spouse from an ultimately sovereign group other than their own.

b) There is a requirement that different ultimately sovereign groups join together for the conduct of important rituals and ceremonies (e.g., rituals for the initiation of the young).

c) One or more ultimately sovereign groups have been united with another by right of conquest.

d) Powerful and conflicting groups in the same society make demands on the same individuals without providing legitimate means for resolving these conflicts.

e) Strong and persistent conflicts of interest are likely to exist between husbands and wives or between the generations. By itself, the existence of a matri-family system is *not* sufficient evidence to satisfy this criterion.

f) Severe and unresolvable conflicts persist between persons who occupy different and widespread social roles in a society; the nature of those diverse roles is the source of the conflict among their occupants.

The coding categories are:

0. Absent
1. Present: fits cases c, d, e, or f above
2. Present: fits cases a or b above

Col. 25: (III) *High God:*

Refers to a spirit who is said to have created all reality and/or is reality's ultimate governor. Includes spirits whose sole act was to create the other spirits who, in turn, produced the natural world.

0. None
1. Present—otiose
2. Present—active in human affairs but no specific support to human morality
3. Present—active in human affairs and gives specific support to human morality
4. Uncertain whether high god is present

Col. 26: (IV) *Superior Gods:*
Code reports number of such gods up to 9 or more.
Spirits who control all phases of one or more, but not all, human activities. Certain classes of spirits are excluded from this column: ancestral spirits, spirits associated with a single, limited place or population (e.g., guardian spirits of particular individuals, spirits attached to a particular mountain or lake or tree or house).

Col. 27: (IV) *Superior Gods:* (Not including those attached to a particular occupational specialty.) Code reports number of such gods up to 9 or more.
Refers to superior gods other than those associated with one particular occupational specialty which is present in the society.

Col. 28: (IV) *Superior Gods of Questionable Authenticity:* Code gives number of such gods up to 9 or more.
Spirits which may be superior gods but which are not described with enough precision to be certain.

Col. 29: (V) *Active Ancestral Spirits:*
0. Absent—dead ancestors do not influence the living

    1. Present—nature of activity unspecified

    2. Present—aid or punish living humans

    3. Present—are invoked by the living to assist in earthly affairs

Col. 30: (VI) *Reincarnation:*

    Refers to the belief that the dead return to life—take on a corporeal existence.

    0. Absent

    1. Present—in human form

    2. Present—in animal form

Col. 31: (VII) *Exuvial Magic:*

    Magic which employs some part or organic product (excreta, spittle) of a human's body as a means of controlling that person or his soul.

    0. Absent

    1. Present

Col. 32: (VII) *Cannibalism:*

    0. Absent

    1. Present

Col. 33: (VII) *Taking of Scalps or Bones of Victims:*

    0. Absent

    1. Present

Col. 34: (VII) *Head-hunting:*

    0. Absent

    1. Present

Col. 35: (VII) *Human Sacrifice:*

    0. Absent

    1. Present

Col. 36: (VIII) *Prevalence of Witchcraft:*

    0. Little or none—ethnographer reports that it is absent or of very minor importance

    1. Some—cases not otherwise coded in this column

    2. Prevalent—ethnographer reports that it is the source of all or much illness or misfortune or that it is a frequent cause of death

    X. Conflicting evidence

Col. 37: (IX) *Supernatural Sanctions for Morality—Effects on Health:*

Refers to rewards or deprivations from supernatural sources (spirit or mana) which are believed to affect an individual because he helped or harmed other members of the same society. Health should include illness or freedom therefrom, life and death, the length of life, malformed offspring. Includes cases in which magical techniques in human hands punish or reward other people, providing that people believe magic was given to them by spirits for the express purpose of aiding the good and punishing the evil.

Does *not* include the following:

a) Magical techniques used by people to help or harm others without the presence of a legitimating myth saying that the spirits gave magic to man for the promotion of good and the suppression of evil.

b) Behavior is subjected to supernatural sanctions without explicit reference to the rationale that the sanctions were imposed because the behavior helped or harmed other people.

c) Persons rewarded or punished do not belong to the same ultimately sovereign group (e.g., use of black magic against alien enemies).

o. Absent or no data

1. Present

Y. Conflicting evidence

Col. 38: (IX) *Supernatural Sanctions for Morality—Effects on Experiences in the Afterlife:*

Includes special pleasures or tortures as consequences of acts which help or harm other people. Includes cases in which special contributions as a warrior, parent, governmental official, or occupant of some other role, or deficiencies in conduct therein, lead to rewards or deprivations in the afterlife. Always includes cases in which the actions of the living are said to affect the comforts which the dead receive. It is assumed that the morality of the deceased when he was alive determines the way his descendants treat his soul after he dies.

0. Absent or no data
1. Present
Y. Conflicting evidence

Col. 39: (IX) *Supernatural Sanctions for Morality—Other Effects:*
Sanctions not coded in Cols. 37 and 38, such as accidents, misfortunes, or mishaps other than those specified under effects on health (e.g., a crop failure).

0. Absent or no data
1. Present
Y. Conflicting evidence

C. Classification of the Sampled Societies

	1	2	3	4	5	6	7	8	9
Arapesh	4	1	0	0	0	2	2	X	0
Arunta	6	1	0	0	0	0	0	0	0
Aymara	5	1	1	1	0	2	Y	Y	1
Azande	5	2	2	3	0	0	2	1	0
Aztec	5	2	1	3	3	1	2	X	1
Bemba	5	2	1	3	1	2	Y	Y	0
Blackfoot	6	3	1	2	0	2	0	2	1
Carib	7	2	1	0	1	2	0	0	0
Carrier	6	1	1	1	0	Y	Y	Y	0
Cuna	5	Y	0	1	1	2	2	Y	1
Dobuans	4	1	1	0	1	2	2	2	Y
Egyptians	5	2	0	3	3	2	2	X	1
Eskimo	6	0	1	0	1	0	0	0	0
Ga	5	2	1	2	2	1	2	2	1
Ganda	9	2	1	3	0	1	2	1	1
Hottentot	2	1	1	1	1	2	1	1	1
Iban	5	2	0	1	1	2	2	Y	1
Ifaluk	9	1	0	1	0	0	0	Y	0
Ifugao	5	Y	2	1	0	2	2	2	1
Iroquois	5	3	1	3	2	0	0	2	0
Israelites	5	2	1	2	2	2	2	2	1
Karen	5	Y	2	1	1	2	Y	X	1
Kaska	1	0	1	0	0	2	2	2	1
Lengua	4	1	1	0	1	0	Y	X	0
Lepcha	8	Y	1	0	0	2	2	2	1
Lozi	5	3	0	3	1	2	0	1	0
Marquesans	9	0	2	2	2	1	2	Y	1
Miao	5	2	1	Y	0	2	0	X	1
Nandi	3	Y	2	2	0	1	0	2	1
Nez Percés	7	3	1	1	1	Y	Y	Y	0
Nuer	5	1	1	3	1	2	0	2	0
Nyakyusa	5	3	1	2	1	2	0	2	0
Orokaiva	4	1	2	0	1	0	Y	2	0
Pomo	0	1	1	0	1	0	2	X	1
Romans	5	3	1	3	3	2	2	Y	1
Samoyed	2	1	1	2	1	2	Y	2	1
Shoshoni	0	0	1	0	0	0	Y	Y	0
Tallensi	5	1	1	2	0	2	0	X	1
Tanala	5	1	2	0	1	2	0	1	1
Timbira	4	Y	2	1	1	1	0	Y	0
Tiv	5	2	2	1	0	2	2	2	1
Toda	3	2	0	0	0	2	2	Y	1
Trumai	7	1	2	0	1	1	0	0	0
Winnebago	8	2	1	1	1	2	0	2	0
Yagua	6	Y	1	0	0	0	0	1	0
Yahgan	0	1	Y	0	0	0	0	1	0
Yokuts	6	1	1	1	1	0	0	2	1
Yurok	1	3	2	0	0	2	2	2	1
Zulu	3	2	1	3	1	2	2	2	0
Zuni	5	2	Y	2	3	0	2	0	0

10	11	12	13	14	15	16	17	18	19	20
0	1	2	9	9	0	3	1	0	0	1
0	5	2	9	9	0	X	0	0	0	0
0	7	3	0	X	0	X	1	1	1	0
0	7	4	4	X	5	X	3	3	0	0
3	9	3	3	7	4	7	6	6	1	1
3	6	4	4	X	5	8	3	3	1	Y
0	7	3	4	X	4	X	2	2	0	0
0	3	3	1	X	1	X	0	0	0	0
0	4	3	4	6	4	6	1	1	1	1
3	7	3	4	X	4	X	2	2	1	0
0	1	2	9	9	1	8	0	0	1	Y
3	9	5	Y	Y	5	X	6	6	Y	0
0	2	2	9	9	1	X	0	0	0	0
0	9	2	9	9	3	X	4	3	1	0
3	9	6	4	5	5	X	6	6	2	0
0	5	2	9	9	4	7	0	0	1	1
0	3	2	9	9	1	X	0	0	0	0
3	3	3	4	7	4	7	1	1	1	1
0	3	2	9	9	0	4	2	1	0	1
0	6	6	1	X	5	7	2	2	2	1
3	4	4	2	X	4	8	2	2	1	Y
0	3	2	9	9	1	X	0	0	0	0
0	3	2	9	9	0	1	1	1	0	1
0	2	2	9	9	1	5	0	0	Y	1
1	Y	3	0	8	0	8	0	0	1	Y
3	9	5	2	X	5	X	2	1	0	0
3	7	2	9	9	2	X	3	1	0	0
3	3	3	0	8	0	8	1	1	1	Y
0	6	3	2	X	2	X	3	3	Y	0
0	3	2	9	9	1	X	0	0	0	0
0	4	6	X	1	2	X	4	4	1	0
0	4	4	1	X	4	X	1	1	1	0
0	2	3	1	8	1	8	0	0	1	Y
3	3	2	9	9	1	X	1	1	0	0
3	9	5	Y	Y	5	X	6	6	0	0
0	3	2	9	9	0	8	0	0	0	Y
0	1	1	9	9	0	0	0	0	0	1
0	4	4	Y	2	4	5	0	0	1	1
0	6	3	4	3	4	3	1	1	1	1
0	9	4	1	X	2	X	6	6	1	0
1	4	3	2	2	2	2	1	1	1	1
0	4	2	9	9	0	5	0	0	1	1
0	5	2	9	9	1	X	0	0	0	0
0	4	2	9	9	1	8	1	1	0	Y
1	3	2	9	9	1	5	1	1	0	1
0	1	1	9	9	0	0	0	0	0	1
0	6	3	4	X	4	X	1	1	0	0
0	3	1	9	9	0	0	0	0	0	1
3	9	4	0	5	5	X	3	3	2	0
1	9	2	9	9	3	7	6	6	1	1

	21	22	23	24	25	26	27	28	29
Arapesh	1	0	0	2	0	0	0	0	3
Arunta	3	0	1	2	0	0	0	0	1
Aymara	0	0	0	2	4	5	5	2	2
Azande	0	0	1	1	3	0	0	0	0
Aztec	1	0	0	0	2	4	2	1	0
Bemba	1	1	0	1	2	1	1	0	3
Blackfoot	0	0	0	0	4	1	1	6	0
Carib	0	2	0	0	1	1	1	5	1
Carrier	0	1	0	2	1	0	0	0	1
Cuna	1	1	0	0	3	2	2	0	0
Dobuans	0	1	1	2	0	1	1	3	1
Egyptians	Y	0	Y	1	3	9	Y	Y	Y
Eskimo	0	0	0	0	0	3	0	5	2
Ga	0	0	0	0	0	3	0	1	3
Ganda	0	0	0	1	1	9	6	4	3
Hottentot	0	0	1	2	0	3	3	1	3
Iban	1	2	0	0	0	3	3	0	0
Ifaluk	1	1	0	0	1	7	5	0	2
Ifugao	0	0	1	2	0	6	6	1	2
Iroquois	1	1	0	0	2	5	5	0	1
Israelites	0	0	1	0	3	Y	Y	Y	2
Karen	0	0	0	0	4	9	9	2	2
Kaska	1	1	0	2	0	0	0	0	2
Lengua	0	Y	0	2	1	0	0	0	0
Lepcha	0	0	1	0	4	3	3	0	0
Lozi	X	0	0	1	1	0	0	0	3
Marquesans	0	2	1	0	0	6	3	3	3
Miao	1	0	1	0	1	3	3	1	2
Nandi	1	0	0	0	4	0	0	2	2
Nez Percés	0	Y	0	2	0	0	0	0	0
Nuer	2	0	0	0	3	2	2	0	2
Nyakyusa	0	0	1	1	1	0	0	0	3
Orokaiva	0	0	0	0	0	0	0	0	3
Pomo	0	1	0	2	4	1	1	5	0
Romans	Y	1	0	0	4	9	Y	Y	0
Samoyed	0	0	0	0	0	2	2	1	0
Shoshoni	0	0	0	2	0	0	0	0	0
Tallensi	0	0	1	0	4	0	0	0	3
Tanala	0	0	1	0	1	0	0	0	3
Timbira	1	1	0	0	0	0	0	2	3
Tiv	0	0	0	1	4	0	0	0	2
Toda	1	2	0	0	0	2	2	0	0
Trumai	0	0	0	2	0	2	2	1	0
Winnebago	2	0	0	0	4	0	0	7	0
Yagua	0	0	0	2	0	0	0	0	1
Yahgan	0	0	0	2	3	1	1	0	1
Yokuts	1	1	0	2	0	0	0	9	1
Yurok	0	0	0	2	4	0	0	0	0
Zulu	2	0	1	1	1	3	3	1	3
Zuni	3	1	0	1	0	2	1	3	3

30	31	32	33	34	35	36	37	38	39
0	1	0	0	1	0	1	0	0	1
1	0	1	0	0	0	2	0	0	0
0	0	0	0	0	0	2	0	0	1
2	0	1	0	0	0	2	1	0	1
0	0	0	0	0	1	1	0	1	1
0	0	0	0	0	0	1	0	0	0
0	0	0	1	0	0	1	1	0	1
0	0	0	0	0	0	0	0	0	0
1	0	0	0	0	0	X	0	0	0
0	0	0	0	0	0	0	0	1	1
0	0	1	0	0	0	2	0	0	1
0	0	0	0	0	0	1	1	1	1
0	1	0	0	0	0	1	1	0	1
1	0	0	0	0	1	0	1	1	1
1	1	0	0	0	1	2	0	1	1
0	1	0	0	0	0	2	0	0	1
0	0	0	0	1	0	1	1	1	1
0	0	0	0	0	0	0	0	0	0
0	0	0	0	1	0	1	1	0	1
0	1	1	1	0	0	1	0	0	X
0	0	0	0	0	0	0	1	X	1
1	0	0	1	0	0	1	0	1	1
1	0	0	1	0	0	1	1	0	1
1	0	0	0	0	0	2	0	0	0
1	1	0	0	0	0	0	1	1	1
0	1	0	0	0	0	2	0	0	0
0	0	1	0	0	0	1	0	1	0
1	0	0	0	0	0	1	1	1	1
1	0	0	0	0	0	1	0	0	1
0	0	0	0	0	0	1	0	0	0
0	0	0	0	0	0	0	1	0	1
0	0	0	0	0	0	2	1	0	1
0	0	1	0	0	0	1	1	0	0
0	1	0	1	0	0	2	0	1	0
0	0	0	0	0	0	1	1	X	1
0	0	0	0	0	0	1	0	X	1
0	0	0	0	0	0	2	0	0	0
0	0	0	0	0	0	0	1	0	1
0	0	0	0	0	0	2	1	1	1
0	0	0	0	0	0	0	0	0	0
0	1	0	0	1	0	2	1	0	1
1	1	0	0	0	0	1	0	0	X
0	0	0	0	0	0	1	0	0	0
1	0	0	0	0	0	1	1	1	1
0	0	0	0	0	0	2	0	0	0
0	0	0	0	0	0	0	1	0	1
0	1	0	1	0	0	2	0	0	0
0	0	0	0	0	0	2	0	0	0
0	1	0	0	0	0	2	1	0	0
0	0	0	1	0	0	2	0	0	1

D. Key to Table XXV

The values given in this table are the probabilities that the pairs of variables concerned are not independent of one another. All probabilities at or beyond the .10 level are reported. The computation from which these probabilities were derived is chi-square.

The signs before these probabilities indicate the direction of the relationship. A plus (+) sign indicates a positive relationship, minus (−) a negative relationship, and curves are used to note positively decelerating (⌢) and negatively accelerating (⌣) relationships.

The variables which correspond to each number in the table's top margin are:

1—Number of sovereign organizations
2—Ratio of number of nonsovereign communal organizations to number of sovereign organizations
3—Number of specialties in communal activities
4—Number of specialties in noncommunal activities
5—Principal source of food
6—Amount of food produced
7—Degree of threat from armed attacks by alien societies
8—Amount of the bride price
9—Debts
10—Social classes
11—Individually owned property
12—Unit of settlement
13—Size of population of ultimately sovereign organization
14—Matri-family organization
15—Presence of primogeniture
16—Number of unorganized social categories
17—Presence of unlegitimated contacts
18—Presence of sovereign kinship groups other than the society or nuclear family
19—Ultimately sovereign group is a kinship organization
20—Pattern of variables used to predict immanence of soul

TABLE XXV

INTERRELATIONS AMONG INDEPENDENT VARIABLES *

	1	2	3	4	5	6	7	8	9	10	11	12	13	14	15	16	17	18	19	20
1		+.001		+.10	+.01	+.05							+.001					+.001		−.001 #
2			+.001	+.02	+.01	+.01						+.05	+.02			+.10		+.02		
3												+.01	+.01						−.01	
4						⌣.05			+.10											
5						+.01					+.02	+.02	+.001			−.10		+.05		
6												+.10	+.01			⌣.10				
7																				
8										+.02	+.10									
9										+.01		.05								
10											+.01				+.10					
11																			−.001	+.001 #
12													+.001							
13																		+.10	−.05	
14																				
15																				
16																				+.01 #
17																				−.10
18																				−.01 #
19																				

* For details consult the Key to this table
\# A defining characteristic of this pattern

APPENDIX II

NOTES ON THE PRIMORDIAL AND CONSTITUTIONAL STRUCTURES

1. The primordial may be the referent in experience of the religious mystic's concept of the "wholly other." Both are infinitely differentiated, yet their parts are united and interdependent. Both are known as vague and chaotic, yet sensible and intricately organized. Both are, withal, consistent in their actions, although this consistency can be detected only over long periods of time.

   Mystics often speak of the inner features of the wholly other—of the Godhead—as somehow beyond good and evil. This, too, is like the contents of the primordial, for it is only after such contents become public and self-conscious that their consequences can be appreciated and responsibility for their enactment can be assigned. Prior to such assignment, they are neither good nor bad, true nor false.

   The mystic must participate in this primordial order and feel his unity in its unity. He must accept its seeming chaos and its amoral structure in order to accept its unity. Such acceptance represents perhaps the deepest possible commitment to a social order and the most thorough involvement of the individual in its processes. We may note that while magic seeks to manipulate the primordial potentialities in the interest of human desires, mysticism seeks to accept the primordial and to unite the individual with it.

2. The "hot" jazz combination and the "hot" intellectual conversation—both spontaneous and free ranging—may get some of their great appeal from their free and easy use of the primordial social relations present in the situation. In both cases, the individuals move in what seem to be very special and individualistic directions, yet, just when it seems the "soloist" must leave the musical theme or the thread of the argument, he comes back and reveals the appropriateness of his performance to the topics of mutual interest. In

both cases, the actors are caught up by the collective task, losing their selves in it, yet using their selves to contribute to it. These social situations reveal easy familiarity with the basic structure of social relations—with the primordial and constitutional structures. This, however, is not a self-conscious familiarity, but an unwitting acquaintanceship. The attraction for participants comes from enhanced understanding of those structures as they are revealed by the explorations of fellow participants. In this sense, then, such social situations are like art which enables us to make public and exterior the motivational side of our experience, yet does not enable us to make the self-conscious analysis of that experience permitted by thorough denotative verbalization. The ability to participate in such social situations is a kind of final indication of the degree to which an individual is a full member of the group.

APPENDIX III

RELIABILITY OF THE CODING

As stated in Chapter II, funds for a test of the code's reliability became available after the data of these studies were analyzed. Two advanced graduate students in anthropology were employed to read the monographic literature originally canvassed and to categorize the information they found by means of the code presented in Appendix I. Neither student was otherwise acquainted with my work or thinking. Because only limited funds were available, these students read the literature describing only 20 of the 50 societies in our sample. The 20 were chosen at random from the original group of 50. Each student read the monographs pertaining to 10 of the 20 societies.

Table XXVI indicates the correspondence between their judgments and my own. This table contains, first, the number of each coded variable assigned to it in Appendix I. Then, three pieces of information follow: the percentage of cases in which one of the students and I were in complete agreement in our coding, a product-moment coefficient of correlation between the students' ratings and those which I employed, and the probability with which a coefficient of that magnitude might have occurred by chance alone.

In the case of 28 of the 39 variables, the students and I agreed in our ratings more often than could be easily accounted for by chance. The 11 variables on which we did not so agree require special attention.

We may look first at the variables numbered 13, 14, 15, and 16. As Appendix I indicates, these are, respectively:

13: Nature of Third Sovereign Organization—Territorial
14: Nature of Third Sovereign Organization—Kinship
15: Nature of Ultimately Sovereign Organization—Territorial
16: Nature of Ultimately Sovereign Organization—Kinship

Inspection of the joint distribution of our ratings indicates that we usually agreed on the presence or absence of a third sovereign organization and whether it was or was not founded on the basis

Appendix III: Reliability of the Coding

TABLE XXVI

RELIABILITY OF CODING

Variable Number	Per Cent Agreement	Coefficient of Correlation	Probability is Less Than:
1	85	.70	.01
2	55	.58	.01
3	35	.31	*
4	75	.68	.01
5	85	.89	.01
6	60	.50	.05
7	70	.45	.05
8	30	.24	*
9	80	.66	.01
10	80	.48	.05
11	25	.83	.01
12	45	.54	.02 **
13	30	.17	*
14	20	−.15	*
15	55	.07	*
16	28	.30	*
17	45	.84	.01
18	40	.84	.01
19	70	.73	.01
20	70	.52	.02
21	50	.51	.05
22	80	.58	.01
23	80	.79	.01
24	75	.62	.01
25	65	.81	.01
26	50	.87	.01
27	70	.93	.01
28	35	.67	.01
29	50	.66	.01
30	95	.88	.01
31	70	.28	*
32	70	.28	*
33	75	.38	*

TABLE XXVI (*continued*)

Variable Number	Per Cent Agreement	Coefficient of Correlation	Probability is Less Than:
34	100	1.00	.01
35	90	.40	*
36	75	.52	.02
37	80	.66	.01
38	65	.39	.10
39	80	.60	.01

* Probability is greater than .10.

** Inter-rater agreement as to whether there were fewer than three sovereign groups as against three or more was 80 per cent. The correlation was .66 which is significant at a level of probability beyond .01.

of kinship as well as territory. We did not, however, concur on the nature of the third sovereign organizations which we said existed, nor on the variety of kin or territorial form taken by ultimately sovereign groups. Our data indicate that these disagreements were rarely due to differences in judgment about the particular group in question. In the case of a given society, for example, both coders would agree that a union of villages was the unit holding ultimate sovereignty. We would also agree that this unit was a kinship organization. We would be likely to disagree, however, on which of the kinship categories to apply to that union and whether it was, territorially speaking, a district or a chiefdom.

The only point in our work at which the distinctions coded for these four variables are of any importance is in Chapter III. Discussing monotheism, we asked whether it might be the *kind* of third or ultimately sovereign group, rather than the *number* of such groups, which produced a belief in a high god. The answer, based on my original coding, was negative. Although my check-coders and I do not agree in our judgments on these variables, the answer to the problem raised in Chapter III would still be negative if we employed their judgments in these matters instead of mine. While this finding does not contradict the results stated in Chapter III, we shall have to await more reliable codes of the varieties of sovereign organizations before being as confident as we might like that it is the number, not the kind, of such groups which is associated with monotheism.

Three other variables, numbers 31, 32, and 33 present us with a different situation. They are: Exuvial Magic, Cannibalism, and Scalping. Together with variable 34 (Head-hunting), these three comprised our indicators for the soul's immanence. In each case, we are dealing with a rather rare event. This means that, although raters may generally agree about the absence of the event, their slightest deviance from consensus concerning its presence destroys the chance of obtaining a significant co-efficient of correlation. As the percentages of agreement indicate, the coders did agree with one another in a substantial majority of the judgments concerning these variables. Fortunately, their disagreements, although sharply depressing the size of the correlations, have no important effect on our findings in the chapter on immanence. Those findings coded the concept of immanence as being present if *any one* of these four indicators was found in a society. The students and I agree in 80 per cent of the cases in which we judge whether one or none of the variables is present, and the coefficient of correlation also shows significant consensus on this score ($r = .66$; $p = < .01$).

A comparable situation appears in connection with variable 38: Supernatural Sanctions for Morality—Effects on Experiences in the Afterlife. In this instance, as in that just discussed, the variable in question was not employed by itself in our work, but was combined with variables 37 and 39 as an indicator of super-natural sanctions for morality. If *any one* of these three was present, such sanctions were considered present. The students and I agree in 85 per cent of our judgments concerning the presence or absence of at least one of these three variables. Again, the coefficient of correlation indicates that there is sig-nificant consensus among us ($r = .67$; $p = < .01$).

Variable 35, Human Sacrifice, need not concern us further. It was not employed in any of our analyses, and was reported in the code merely because it had been assessed.

Two variables remain for discussion. They are number 3

(Degree of Threat from Armed Attacks by Alien Societies), and 8 (Amount of the Bride Price).

The students and I do not agree in our coding of these variables. Although neither plays a crucial role in the studies reported in this book, the likely reasons for our inability to achieve consensus are of some interest for future investigations.

In retrospect, our great difficulty in connection with the degree to which societies are threatened by armed attack from without seems due to differences in frame of reference—differences not corrected by explicit coding instructions. The students assumed that warfare usually has little significance for primitive life. This judgment is founded on the well documented observation that primitives engage in many raids, but in few wars which involve large-scale damage to life or property. By contrast, I tended to assume that the frequency of armed conflict, and the uncertainty of its outcome, should receive greater weight. The result was wide disagreement between us.

More surprising is our lack of consensus on the amount paid for brides in these societies. The difficulty here seems to lie in our disagreement about the amount, not its presence or absence. Not only do we disagree with each other in this matter, but also with ratings provided on this subject by Murdock.[1] It is evident that future studies which require observations of these matters must greatly refine existing codes to obtain reliable results.

In summary, on almost all codes of importance for an interpretation of our findings, the students and I achieved a significant degree of agreement. This agreement, though far from perfect, is great enough to make it unlikely that major predictions were falsely confirmed or disconfirmed as a result of an unreliable code. The exceptions are the four codes concerning the nature of third sovereign organizations and ultimately sovereign organizations.

NOTES

1. Bronislaw Malinowski, "Magic, Science, and Religion," in his *Magic, Science, and Religion and Other Essays* (Glencoe, Illinois: The Free Press, 1948), 1–71.
2. This conception is related to Plato's notion of immaterial essences which lie behind the appearances of reality.
3. Some brief mention should be given to certain additional descriptions of the origin of religion or the supernatural. These are identified below with authors who made them famous.

    Andrew Lang, *The Making of Religion* (London: Longmans, Green, and Co., 1909). This pioneer student of religion's beginnings pictured the sequence of stages by which he believed religion had evolved since prehistoric times. He professed ignorance, however, of the sources of the "fundamental" beliefs possessed by all religions (p. 301). His evolutionary scheme has not received empirical support.

    William G. Sumner and Albert G. Keller, *The Science of Society*, vol. 2 (New Haven: Yale University Press, 1927). Following Sumner's argument as developed in his book *Folkways* (1907), these authors propose that primitive religion springs from a juncture of ghost-fear and chance. Men, they say, inferred the existence of ghosts from experiences of death, fantasy, and dreams. Simultaneously, they lived in a world in which much seemed to occur by chance —that is, in which much was inexplicable. Primitives, they continue, attributed ill luck to behaviors which offended the ghosts. The elements of this position are discussed and rejected in our textual presentation.

    Sigmund Freud, *The Future of an Illusion* (London:

Permission of Horace Liveright, © 1928). Freud argues that the individual finds much of life hard to endure. If, however, "the elements have passions that rage like those in our own souls, if death itself is not something spontaneous, but the violent act of an evil will, if everywhere in nature we have about us beings who resemble those of our own environment, then indeed we can . . . deal psychically with our frantic anxiety. . . . we can have recourse to the same methods against these violent supermen of the beyond that we make use of in our own community; we can try to exorcise them, to appease them, to bribe them, and so rob them of part of their power by thus influencing them." And it is not difficult for men to adopt this strategy of personifying and then manipulating natural forces for "there is nothing new in this situation. It has an infantile prototype, and is really only the continuation of this. For once before one has been in such a state of helplessness; as a little child in one's relationship to one's parents." But the onward march of empirical knowledge destroys the supernatural.

"In the course of time the first observations of law and order in natural phenomena are made, and therewith the forces of nature lose their human traits."

In contrast to many other writers, Freud does try to explain why men's response to fearful and uncontrollable happenings should take the form of supernatural beliefs. First, he suggests that natural explanations are unavailable. Secondly, he proposes a psychological mechanism—the generalization of conceptions once developed by the individual to cope with his parents—which leads men to personify dangerous and unknown forces in the world. Just as the parents were once conceived as all-powerful and immortal, and as exercising an invisible supervision over the child's thoughts, so the unknown forces of nature and society are now conceived by adults as having the same properties.

Freud's interpretation indicates how ideas of spirits might appear. It does not seem to explain the existence of mana.

Of greater importance, and irrespective of the merits of Freud's psychological assumptions, his scheme runs counter to certain observations about beliefs in spirits. First, it appears that significant changes in such beliefs have occurred without being preceded by important and widespread changes in the relations of parents and children. Our information about this subject may be faulty, but existing studies picture a sequence which should not occur if our ideas about supernatural beings were generalizations from experiences in infancy. Second, primitives do not always explain terrifying and overwhelming natural forces as the action of spirits nor do they attribute terrifying and overwhelming characteristics to all spirits. Again, our information may be in error, but, such as it is, it does not fit Freud's assumptions. Finally, evidence from the investigations described in these chapters is consistent with the judgment that some, but not all, of the potent forces which men experience are conceived by people as spirits. The implications of this finding for Freud's interpretation are reviewed in Chapter X.

John Dewey, "The Religious in Experience," in Joseph Ratner (ed.), *Intelligence in the Modern World: John Dewey's Philosophy* (New York: The Modern Library, 1939), 1003–37, considered the essential nature of religious experience to be the feeling of integration with one's self and with others. Since this view and the similar position of George H. Mead, [see his *Mind, Self and Society* (Chicago: The University of Chicago Press, 1934), 273–98], change the meaning of religion from that presented in this chapter, they are not discussed further.

4. Robert H. Lowie, *Primitive Religion* (New York: Permission of Boni and Liveright, © 1948), xvi–xvii.

5. Edward B. Tylor, *Primitive Culture, Researches into the Development of Mythology, Philosophy, Religion, Language, Art and Custom*, vol. 2 (New York: Harper and Bros., 1948). Originally published in 1871.

6. Emile Durkheim, *The Elementary Forms of the Religious Life, A Study in Religious Sociology*, Joseph W. Swain, trans. (London: George Allen and Unwin, Ltd., n.d.), 37. Originally published in 1912.

7. Talcott Parsons, "The Theoretical Development of the

Sociology of Religion," in his *Essays in Sociological Theory Pure and Applied* (Glencoe, Illinois: The Free Press, 1949), 52–66.

8. Lowie, *op. cit.*, 155.

9. Since I have neither reported nor employed Durkheim's applications of this scheme to the special case of Australian totemism, the familiar critiques of that application are not reviewed here. They are found in *ibid.*, 157–63. Other critical points mentioned by Lowie, namely that Durkheim's position identifies society with the crowd, or is incompatible with instances in which major natural phenomena are deified, or with the fact of individual religious experience, have also been left undiscussed. Such criticisms reflect misunderstanding of Durkheim's argument and its implications. A recent review of commentaries on Durkheim is given by Imogen Seger in her monograph *Durkheim and His Critics on the Sociology of Religion* (New York: Columbia University, Bureau of Applied Social Research, 1957).

10. The conception of sovereignty in a variety of groups was developed most fully by the pluralists. For a summary of their position and a good bibliography, see: Francis W. Coker, "Pluralism," *Encyclopaedia of the Social Sciences*, vol. 12 (New York: The Macmillan Co., 1934), 170–74.

11. The phrase "is likely" was chosen over some more positive phrase because one cannot rule out the possibility that conditions other than sovereignty may produce the same result. Since my thinking moved from the idea of "spirits" to the social conditions which seem to embody the characteristics of spirits, I have not been forced to examine in detail the logical or psychological grounds by which an experience of sovereignty might lead to beliefs in *personified* supernatural realities. This reversed approach, while not necessary for these studies, presents interesting and difficult problems which a fuller account of religion must solve. As a temporary explanation, I would propose:

a). Men associate purposing with the behavior of human individuals.

b). When they find themselves in the grip of unseen and

  nonhuman purposing agents, men tend to think of those agents as superhuman persons.

12. A legitimate social relationship is one in which the participants believe that the nature of their contacts with one another is right and just.

13. The most detailed discussion of character in the individual is Wilhelm Reich's *Character-Analysis*, T. P. Wolfe, trans. (New York: Orgone Institute, 1945). See also: Otto Fenichel, *The Psychoanalytic Theory of Neurosis* (New York: W. W. Norton, 1945).

14. Readers of the psychoanalytic literature may notice affinities between Freud's concept of the primary process and the primordial social relations described here. This pair of ideas may be considered as isomorphic despite the difference in their empirical referents. In both cases we deal with a set of active relationships which are hidden from the organs of consciousness. In social life, such organs may be equated with the constitutional structures. Neither the primary process nor the primordial relations ever become fully public. Further, their components are unaware of their own internal connections and of the total pattern which they comprise. Separated from the constitutional structures (the social ego) and the ideal (the social superego), they exhibit many of the qualities which Freud attributes to primary process. They are not ordered or rationalized with respect to the operation of the constitutional structures. They are not regulated by having to be confronted with their consequences for public action. They are not ordered by being confronted with the fact that their consequences conflict with one another. They are not curbed by the perception that certain stages are required for their being put into effect—in this sense they are atemporal. They follow the paths which lead to the greatest likelihood of realization in public policy, ordered only by their own strength and by the likelihood of such realization. They seem almost indestructible —their roots being nourished constantly and reality never intervening to reveal their flaws. Those who participate in these relationships exhibit no doubts, negations, or varying

degrees of certainty concerning them. Perhaps, like the primary process, these primordial relations are easily condensed or displaced.

15. The distinction between magic and religion given here differs from some others in the literature. Thus Marion J. Levy in *The Structure of Society* (Princeton: Princeton University Press, 1952), 243–44, 336, defines magic as the use of nonempirical means to achieve empirical ends; religion as the use of nonempirical means to gain nonempirical ends. This would place a prayer for health under the category of magic and a prayer to free souls from purgatory under the heading of religion. It would be impossible to classify situations in which empirical means, such as an offering of food, are used to gain nonempirical ends, such as a pleasant afterlife for deceased relatives. The definitions we shall use distinguish between magic and religion on the basis of the entities they govern, not the means by which those relationships are established or the ends which they are designed to accomplish.

16. See Appendix II for some speculations about the relations of these properties to the idealized properties of supernatural and moral conceptions and to mystical experiences of the godhead.

17. Our use of the term magic should be distinguished from the meaning commonly given in psychoanalysis to "magical thought." In psychoanalysis, magical thinking refers to ideas which the individual would recognize as invalid if he were being as fully rational as "normal" members of his society. By contrast, magical practices with reference to the supernatural are considered in most primitive societies to be completely rational. They are performed by normal adults, and beliefs concerning them have met the test of public acceptance.

NOTES TO CHAPTER II

1. George P. Murdock in a personal communication.
2. George P. Murdock, "The Comparative Study of Cultures," dittoed manuscript. A revised version appears in his "World Ethnographic Sample," *American Anthropologist*, 59 (Au-

gust, 1957), 664–87. Our investigations employed the original dittoed version of this paper.

3. I am indebted for this assistance to David F. Aberle, Richard K. Beardsley, Horace M. Miner, William D. Schorger, El-man R. Service, and Leslie A. White.

4. Albert Cafagna and David Kaplan.

5. Morris Zelditch, Jr., "Role Differentiation in the Nuclear Family: A Comparative Study," in Talcott Parsons and Robert F. Bales, *Family, Socialization and Interaction Process* (Glencoe, Illinois: The Free Press, 1955), 317.

6. From the Ford Foundation Behavioral Science Research Fund established at The University of Michigan.

7. Richard Frucht and Thomas G. Harding.

8. Murdock, "World Ethnographic Sample," *loc. cit.*

9. This last stipulation is modified from one proposed in Raoul Naroll's "A Preliminary Index of Social Development," *The American Anthropologist*, 58 (August, 1956), 687–715.

10. The employment of categories for principal sources of food has been common in anthropology. It was early recognized that these categories provided one index of wealth and the resources from which still more social complexity and wealth might be constructed. Most authors propose that methods of food gathering be arranged in something like the following order of ascending efficiency and resultant wealth: collecting and gathering, hunting and fishing, herding and other pastoral pursuits, raising root crops, and raising grain crops. It is commonly observed that settled agriculture in which grain crops provide the staple food affords significantly more wealth than the other procedures in the list. Thus C. Daryll Forde, in his *Habitat, Economy and Society, A Geographical Introduction to Ethnology* (London: Methuen and Co., Ltd., 1934), 418, declared: "The root crops and fruits . . . did not, however, provide the main food basis of the higher civilizations. . . . The reward of cereal cultivation is greater than of any other form of agriculture. The gathering and threshing of grain is less laborious than the digging of roots; the food value is considerably greater for a given bulk; further, the product can be stored easily and will remain in perfect condition for very long periods.

Surpluses can thus be accumulated to protect dense populations against crop failures." The first extensive and systematic use of such categories was made in Leonard T. Hobhouse, G. C. Wheeler, and Morris Ginsberg, *The Material Culture and Social Institutions of the Simpler Peoples* (London: Chapman and Hall, 1915).

11. The whole problem of estimating the population of primitive and ancient communities is reviewed in Sol Tax and Others (eds.), *An Appraisal of Anthropology Today* (Chicago: The University of Chicago Press, 1953), 240–45. The estimate of five living persons in a nuclear family at any particular time is admittedly arbitrary, but is based on the average number of people in such groups as reported for a number of societies. This figure is also used in H. S. and C. B. Cosgrove, "The Swarts Ruin, A Typical Mimbres Site in Southwestern New Mexico," *Papers of the Peabody Museum of American Archaeology and Ethnology*, 15, no. 1 (Harvard University, 1932), 100–103.

12. A statistically significant finding is one that could not have occurred easily by chance alone. In these chapters, results are called significant if they are marked enough, where evaluated statistically, to occur by chance alone in five or fewer times out of 100 repetitions of the study.

13. This ratio is described in J. E. Keith Smith, "Multi-variate Attribute Analysis," Engineering Research Institute, University of Michigan, August, 1953, and in Alexander M. Mood, *Introduction to the Theory of Statistics* (New York: McGraw-Hill, 1950), 152–64.

NOTES TO CHAPTER III

1. Paul Radin, *Monotheism Among Primitive Peoples* (London: George Allen and Unwin, Ltd., 1924), 15–16.

2. For a summary of Schmidt's position and references to more detailed presentations of the evidence, see: Wilhelm Schmidt, *The Origin and Growth of Religion, Facts and Theories*, H. J. Rose, trans. (London: Methuen and Co., Ltd., 1935).

3. *Ibid.*, 283–84.

4. Radin, *op. cit.*

5. *Ibid.*, 65. An argument related to Radin's states that monotheism and certain other theologies are more elaborate than
   alternative beliefs, hence must be the products of professional clergymen. Our data show that monotheistic ideas
   (and most of the other theological notions investigated in
   these chapters) can appear in societies which lack persons
   who specialize in religion. In any case, we know that ideas
   which are not consistent with people's experience are not
   accepted by them. This means that even if religious specialists proposed a theology, its acceptance would depend on
   people who had experienced a world which "fit" that theology. This would lead us, once more, to search for the conditions which were consistent with the proposed theology.
6. James H. Breasted, *The Dawn of Conscience* (New York:
   Charles Scribner's Sons, 1933), 272–302.
7. As explained in Note 9 of Chapter II, this statistic indicates
   the likelihood of a difference occurring by chance alone. In
   this particular case we may say that, were our study repeated
   10,000 times, a difference as large as that shown in Table I
   could occur simply by chance only five times in the 10,000
   repetitions. In other words, it is very unlikely that the relations shown in Table I occurred only by chance.
8. A coefficient of contingency measures the extent to which
   two things increase or decrease together. The corrected coefficient may have any value from +1.00 through .00 to
   −1.00. A coefficient of +1.00 would indicate that as one
   condition, call it X, increased a specified amount, the
   other condition, call it Y, also increased a specified amount.
   A coefficient of −1.00 would indicate that increases in
   X always coincide perfectly with decreases in Y. A coefficient
   of .00 would indicate that the value of X had no relation to
   that of Y. Where a plus (+) sign would precede a coefficient, it is customary to omit that sign.
9. A review of monotheism in ancient Egypt appears in: Leslie
   A. White, "Ikhnaton: The Great Man vs. the Culture
   Process," in his *The Science of Culture, A Study of Man
   and Civilization* (New York: Farrar, Straus and Co., 1949),
   233–81. On monotheism before Ikhnaton, see especially
   pages 254–56.

10. For both tails of the probability distribution.
11. Consult Forde, *op. cit.*
12. We may note, in passing, that our account of monotheism provides an explanation of Israelite beliefs which does not require the postulation of such fictive histories as that of Sigmund Freud's *Moses and Monotheism*, Katherine Jones, trans. (New York: Alfred A. Knopf, 1939).

NOTES TO CHAPTER IV

1. It would be interesting, if only to round out our efforts to understand the origin of various types of spirits, were we able to attempt an explanation of those deities who do not take the form of high gods, superior gods, ancestral spirits, or reincarnated humans. Unfortunately, we have not found any reliable means to isolate and distinguish among the myriad remaining varieties of deity. Too many ethnographers give such scant accounts that we could not develop and apply a reasonably clear classification from their reports. Perhaps other researchers can find ways to circumvent this difficulty.

2. As Melford Spiro reminds us, superior gods *preside* over specialized activities. They do not *merely* "represent" those activities. Thus a god of carpenters is not just a supernatural carpenter, nor does he necessarily do what human carpenters do. A god of carpenters does for human carpenters what such men cannot readily do for themselves.

3. Therefore, all statistical tests in this chapter report the probability for both tails of the distribution.

4. The probability for the relationship with the number of communal specialties is $< .30$.

5. This table uses the purged list of superior gods; that is, it omits deities associated with particular occupational specialties.

6. Readers familiar with the literature contrasting the social philosophies of Roman Catholicism and Calvinism will find many similarities between those views of society and the perspectives outlined here. It may be that social conditions like those sketched in these paragraphs will help to

account for some of the differences in Catholic and Calvinist outlook.

7. Once again, the calculation employs the purged list of superior gods.

NOTES TO CHAPTER V

1. On the nature and universality of the nuclear family consult: George P. Murdock, *Social Structure* (New York: The Macmillan Co., 1949), 1–22 and Melford E. Spiro, "Is the Family Universal?" *American Anthropologist*, 56 (October, 1954), 839–46.

2. When kin groups are also sovereign over territorial units subordinate to the ultimately sovereign unit, something like this same problem may appear. Presumably, however, the distinction between the two organizational principles—kinship and territory—is less sharp in such cases. For that reason, we shall expect the kinship principle, with all its well-known connections to the emotional life of members, to be superordinate, and shall predict that dead ancestors will be active in human experience.

3. Relevant information appears in Baldwin Spencer and F. J. Gillen, *The Arunta, A Study of a Stone Age People*, vol. 1 (London: Macmillan and Co., Ltd., 1927), 72–80, 306–14.

4. Alfred L. Kroeber, *Handbook of the Indians of California*, Smithsonian Institution, Bureau of American Ethnology, Bulletin 78 (Washington, D. C.: U. S. Government Printing Office, 1925), 474.

5. In a personal communication.

6. Sumner and Keller, *op. cit.*

NOTES TO CHAPTER VI

1. A great many of these are reviewed in Ernest W. Burgess and Harvey J. Locke, *The Family, From Institution to Companionship* (New York: American Book Company, 1953), 289–314.

2. Wilfred B. Grubb, *An Unknown People in an Unknown Land* (London: Seeley, Service, and Co., Ltd., 1913), 121.

3. An especially helpful presentation of the philosophy of re-

birth and its setting in the development of the Upanishads is given in Walter Ruben, *Die Philosophen der Upanischaden* (Bern: A. Francke, 1947). Descriptions of the nature of reincarnation beliefs in contemporary India and of the Indian village are found in the following, and in works listed in their bibliographies: S. C. Dube, *Indian Village* (London: Routledge and Kegan Paul Ltd., 1955); McKim Marriott (ed.), *Village India, Studies in the Little Community* (Chicago: The University of Chicago Press, 1955); M. N. Srinivas, *Religion and Society among the Coorgs of South India* (Oxford: The Clarendon Press, 1952).

4. One is reminded in this description that many primitive societies treat one or more occupational or ritual specialties in a similar fashion. Thus it is not uncommon for the blacksmiths or traders in a primitive culture to live off somewhat to themselves and to be partly segregated from other people by ritual prohibitions and requirements. Perhaps we should think of the Indian case as a greatly extended and elaborated instance of the same underlying tendencies.

NOTES TO CHAPTER VII

1. Ralph Linton, "Marquesan Culture," in Abram Kardiner, *The Individual and His Society, The Psychodynamics of Primitive Social Organization* (New York: Columbia University Press, 1939), 142.

2. Gluckman provides a detailed account of the unstable politics of many primitive "conquest" states. See: Max Gluckman, *Custom and Conflict in Africa* (Glencoe, Illinois: The Free Press, 1955), 27–53. For a description of conditions under which such states seem to have greater political stability, see the following: Karl Polanyi, "Marketless Trading in Hammurabi's Time," and A. L. Oppenheim, "A Bird's-Eye View of Mesopotamian Economic History," both in Karl Polanyi, Conrad M. Arensberg, and Harry W. Pearson (eds.), *Trade and Market in the Early Empires* (Glencoe, Illinois: The Free Press, 1957), 12–26, 27–37.

3. Francis Haines, *Red Eagles of the Northwest, The Story of Chief Joseph and His People* (Portland, Oregon: The Scholastic Press, 1939), 252, 282. See also: Helen A. How-

ard and Dan L. McGrath, *War Chief Joseph* (Caldwell, Idaho: The Caxton Printers, Ltd., 1941), 157–58, 220.

4. This probability is for both tails of the distribution.

NOTES TO CHAPTER VIII

1. Monica Wilson, "Witch Beliefs and Social Structure," *The American Journal of Sociology*, 56 (January, 1951), 313; Godfrey and Monica Wilson, *The Analysis of Social Change* (Cambridge: Cambridge University Press, 1945), 89–104.

2. Clyde Kluckhohn, "Navaho Witchcraft," *Papers of the Peabody Museum of American Archaeology and Ethnology*, 22, no. 2 (Harvard University, 1944).

3. *Ibid.*, 47.

4. *Ibid.*, 49.

5. *Ibid.*, 50.

6. *Ibid.*, 51.

7. *Ibid.*, 51–52.

8. *Ibid.*, 63.

9. *Ibid.*

10. *Ibid.*

11. *Ibid.*, 60.

12. It is important for understanding witchcraft to remember that it assumes evil *human* purposes to be at work in the realm of supernature. This is quite different from a belief that harm comes from evil supernatural beings, such as demons, or that a deity both good and evil has caused one's misfortunes. One implication of these considerations is that any derivation of witchcraft from the presence of hardship or evil in human experience must be inadequate. One could as easily derive a belief in evil spirits from such considerations. Instead, one wants to explain why human purposes are involved.

13. The Navahos' situation contains instances of both types of unlegitimated social contacts discussed in Chapter VII. Not only do they possess the deep ambivalences toward one another which their marriage practices evoke, but the integrity of their society is disturbed by the acculturative forces of employment in American enterprises, education in American schools, service in the American armed forces, and

participation in governmental organs formulated and supervised by Americans.

14. Robert H. Lowie, *Primitive Religion* (New York: Boni and Liveright, 1924), 37.

15. A recent and useful survey of the circumstances appears in Timothy D. Ellard's "Salem Witchcraft, A Socio-Anthropological Study," Senior Thesis, Department of Social Relations, Harvard College, 1956.

16. In their study of child training in 75 primitive societies, Whiting and Child find that beliefs in sorcerers as a cause of illness are significantly related to the severity with which youngsters are socialized in connection with oral, sexual, and aggressive behaviors. It would be interesting to explore the possibility that our indicators of unlegitimated and uncontrolled dependencies would, in turn, predict where such beliefs and such methods of child training would appear. Unfortunately only ten of our societies also appear in Whiting and Child's sample and, although those authors note the presence of beliefs that illness is caused by sorcery, they do not tell us whether most illness, or only occasional instances of bad health, are attributed to this cause. These facts prevent an immediate test of connections between our indicators and theirs, but do not preclude gathering new information for that purpose. See: John W. M. Whiting and Irvin L. Child, *Child Training and Personality: A Cross-Cultural Study* (New Haven: Yale University Press, 1953), chap. 12.

17. After this chapter was written, Beatrice Whiting's fine study of *Paiute Sorcery* (New York: The Viking Fund, Inc., 1950) was brought to my attention. Mrs. Whiting found a positive and significant relationship between the importance of sorcery as an explanation of illness and the absence of special authorities empowered to punish offenses or settle disputes. Her data come from a sample of 50 primitive societies.

Her interpretation of this finding is related to our own account of witchcraft. Both explanations find witchcraft associated with the absence of legitimate, objective, and public controls over important social relations. The explana-

˙tion given in the present chapter seems, however, somewhat more general than that of Mrs. Whiting.

Redfield's account of witchcraft in Yucatan also seems to be a special case of our interpretation. He studied four communities, varying in size and urbanization and in degree of contact with the modern world. He shows that, as urbanization increases so does the likelihood that people will attribute illness or ill fortune to the action of witches. Redfield says that the prevalence of witchcraft is "related to the incompletely organized and secularized culture. It seems to us that the weakness of familial and community organization [in urbanized communities] and the incompleteness of a cultural organization are specially manifest in the realm of sickness, in the frequent suspicion of witchcraft, and in the importance of quarreling. . . ." From Robert Redfield, *The Folk Culture of Yucatan* (Chicago: The University of Chicago Press, 1941), 330–31.

NOTES TO CHAPTER IX

1. Tylor, *op. cit.*, chaps. 11 through 17.
2. (New York: F. S. Crofts and Co., 1939).
3. Reo F. Fortune, "Manus Religion," *Memoirs of the American Philosophical Society*, 3 (1935), 357.
4. Bronislaw Malinowski, *The Foundations of Faith and Morals, An Anthropological Analysis of Primitive Beliefs and Conduct with Special Reference to the Fundamental Problems of Religion and Ethics* (London: Oxford University Press, 1935), viii.
5. *Ibid.*, 25.
6. Ralph Linton, "Universal Ethical Principles: An Anthropological View," in Ruth N. Anshen (ed.), *Moral Principles of Action* (New York: Harper and Bros., 1952), 645–60.
7. Malinowski, *The Foundations of Faith and Morals*, 3.
8. *Ibid.*, 6–7.
9. Probability given for both tails of the distribution.
10. Probability given for both tails of the distribution.
11. Wallis, *op. cit.*, 205.
12. David M. Schneider, "Political Organization, Supernatural Sanctions and the Punishment of Incest on Yap," *American*

Anthropologist, 59 (October, 1957), 791–800.

13. Richard B. Brandt, *Hopi Ethics, A Theoretical Analysis* (Chicago: The University of Chicago Press, 1954); John Ladd, *The Structure of a Moral Code, A Philosophical Analysis of Ethical Discourse Applied to the Ethics of the Navaho Indians* (Cambridge: Harvard University Press, 1956).

14. Julia S. Brown, "A Comparative Study of Deviations from Sexual Mores," *American Sociological Review,* 17 (April, 1952), 135–46.

15. These are primarily instances of sexual intercourse between husband and wife during menstruation or at some point during or shortly after pregnancy.

16. *Ibid.,* 144.

17. A study by Spiro of relations between methods of child rearing and the conditions under which spirits act nurturantly or punitively suggests further avenues for research. See: Melford E. Spiro and Roy G. D'Andrade, "A Cross-Cultural Study of Some Supernatural Beliefs," *American Anthropologist,* 60 (June, 1958), 456–66.

NOTES TO CHAPTER X

1. Exploratory studies in a random half of our sample of societies suggest a similar realism in the belief that demons are prevalent and/or potent. Demons were defined as spirits who were not dead ancestors and who sought, without "good cause" or moral justification, to harm men. The data show a significant relationship between a belief in the incidence and/or power of such spirits and the ratio of noncommunal specialties to communal specialties. This may be interpreted, following the discussions in Chapter IV, to mean that demons abound where the socially divisive forces inherent in certain desired roles (the noncommunal specialties) are not counter-balanced by agencies which provide a formal representation for legitimate, public purposes (the communal specialties).

2. Other data on this topic are presented in Michael Argyle's work on *Religious Behaviour* (Glencoe, Illinois: The Free Press, 1959), 140–77.

3. As Note 1 above indicates, even the presence of demons—of wholly evil spirits—seems to conform to this judgment.

4. Some particularly valuable material on this topic appears in Leopold von Wiese and Howard Becker, *Systematic Sociology on the Basis of the Beziehungslehre and Gebildelehre* (New York: John Wiley and Sons, Inc., 1932), 221–27, 316–47, 627–29. See also the following for other approaches: B. Groethuysen, "Secularism," *The Encyclopaedia of the Social Sciences*, vol. 13 (New York: The Macmillan Co., 1934), 631–34; J. Richard Spann (ed.), *The Christian Faith and Secularism* (New York: Abingdon-Cokesbury Press, 1948); J. Milton Yinger, *Religion, Society and the Individual, An Introduction to the Sociology of Religion* (New York: The Macmillan Co., 1957), 118–24.

5. Philip Rieff, "Introduction to Max Weber: 'Science as a Vocation,'" *Daedalus* (Winter [sic], 1958), 111.

6. Philip Selznick, *Leadership in Administration* (Evanston: Row, Peterson and Co., 1957).

7. This topic is discussed in: Guy E. Swanson, "The Effectiveness of Decision-Making Groups," *Adult Leadership*, 8 (June, 1959), 48–52.

NOTE TO APPENDIX III

1. Murdock, *op. cit.* A few other comparisons were possible between Murdock's code and our own. In each case, there is significant agreement. The full sample of 50 societies was employed in these computations:

Col. 1 (Principal source of food): $r = .73; p = < .01$.
Col. 5 (Unit of settlement): $r = .42; p = < .01$.
Col. 22 (Matri-family): $r = .63; p = < .01$.

SELECTED BIBLIOGRAPHY

Key to Abbreviations of Common Titles:

AA: *American Anthropologist.*

APAMNH: *Anthropological Papers of the American Museum of Natural History.*

APS: Meyer Fortes and E. E. Evans-Pritchard (eds.), *African Political Systems* (London: Oxford University Press, 1940).

ARBAE: *Annual Report of the Bureau of American Ethnology* (Washington, D. C.: U. S. Government Printing Office).

HIC: Alfred L. Kroeber, *Handbook of the Indians of California*, Smithsonian Institution, Bureau of American Ethnology, Bulletin 78 (Washington, D. C.: U. S. Government Printing Office, 1925).

HSAI: Julian H. Steward (ed.), *Handbook of South American Indians*, 2 vols., Smithsonian Institution, Bureau of American Ethnology (Washington, D. C.: U. S. Government Printing Office, 1946).

MAAA: *Memoirs of the American Anthropological Association.*

MAES: *Monographs of the American Ethnological Society* (New York: J. J. Augustin, Publisher).

PPMAAE: *Papers of the Peabody Museum of American Archaeology and Ethnology.*

STBCA: Elizabeth Colson and Max Gluckman (eds.), *Seven Tribes of British Central Africa* (London: Oxford University Press, 1951).

UCPAAE: *University of California Publications in American Archaeology and Ethnology.*

ARAPESH

Fortune, Reo F., "Law and Force in Papuan Societies," AA, 49 (April–June, 1947), 244–59.

Mead, Margaret, "The Mountain Arapesh," APAMNH, 36, pt. 3 (1938).

ARUNTA

Elkin, Adolphus P., *The Australian Aborigines, How to Understand Them* (Sydney: Angus and Robertson Ltd., 1954).

Spencer, Baldwin and F. J. Gillen, *The Arunta, A Study of a Stone Age People*, 2 vols. (London: Macmillan and Co., Ltd., 1927).

Strehlow, Theodor G. H., *Aranda Traditions* (Melbourne: Melbourne University Press, 1947).

AYMARA

La Barre, Weston, "The Aymara Indians of the Lake Titicaca Plateau, Bolivia," AA, 50, pt. 2 (January, 1948), 1–250.

Tschopik, Harry, Jr., "The Aymara," HSAI, 2, 501–73.

Tschopik, Harry, Jr., "The Aymara of Chucuito, Peru, 1. Magic," APAMNH, 44, pt. 2 (1951).

AZANDE

Baxter, Paul T. W., *The Azande and Related Peoples of the Anglo-Egyptian Sudan and Belgian Congo* (London: International African Institute, 1953).

Evans-Pritchard, Edward E., *Witchcraft, Oracles and Magic among the Azande* (Oxford: The Clarendon Press, 1937).

Schlippe, Pierre de, *Shifting Cultivation in Africa, The Zande System of Agriculture* (London: Routledge and Kegan Paul Ltd., 1956).

AZTEC

Vaillant, George C., *Aztecs of Mexico: Origin, Rise and Fall of the Aztec Nation* (Garden City, N. Y.: Doubleday, Doran and Co., Inc., 1944).

BEMBA

Richards, Audrey I., *Hunger and Work in a Savage Tribe, A Functional Study of Nutrition among the Southern Bantu* (London: G. Routledge and Sons, Ltd., 1932).

Richards, Audrey I., *Land, Labour and Diet in Northern Rhodesia, An Economic Study of the Bemba Tribe* (London: Oxford University Press, 1939).

Richards, Audrey I., "The Political System of the Bemba Tribe —Northeastern Rhodesia," APS, 83–120.

Richards, Audrey I., "The Bemba of North-Eastern Rhodesia," STBCA, 164–93.

BLACKFOOT

Ewers, John C., *The Horse in Blackfoot Indian Culture*, Smithsonian Institution, Bureau of American Ethnology, Bulletin 159 (Washington, D. C.: U. S. Government Printing Office, 1955).

Goldfrank, Esther S., "Changing Configurations in the Social Organization of a Blackfoot Tribe During the Reserve Period," MAES, 8 (1945), v–73.

Lewis, Oscar, "The Effects of White Contact upon Blackfoot Culture, with Special Reference to the Role of the Fur Trade," MAES, 6 (1942), v–73.

McClintock, Walter, *The Old North Trail, Life, Legends and Religion of the Blackfeet Indians* (London: Macmillan and Co., Ltd., 1910).

Schultz, James W., *My Life as an Indian, The Story of a Red Woman and a White Man in the Lodges of the Blackfeet* (Boston: Houghton Mifflin Co., 1906).

Wissler, Clark, "Ceremonial Bundles of the Blackfoot Indians," APAMNH, 7, pt. 2 (1912), 65–298.

Wissler, Clark, "Social Organization and Ritualistic Ceremonies of the Blackfoot Indians," APAMNH, 7 (New York: American Museum of Natural History, 1912), 1–64.

Wissler, Clark and D. C. Duvall, "Mythology of the Blackfoot Indians," APAMNH, 2, pt. 1 (1908), 1–163.

CARRIER

Goldman, Irving, "The Alkatcho Carrier of British Columbia," in Ralph Linton (ed.), *Acculturation in Seven American Indian Tribes* (New York: D. Appleton-Century, 1940), 333–89.

Jenness, Diamond, "Indians of Canada," *Bulletin of the Canada Department of Mines*, 65 (1932), 363–68.

COPPER ESKIMO
Jenness, Diamond, "The Copper Eskimos," *The Geographical Review*, 4 (August, 1917), 81–91.

Jenness, Diamond, "The Life of the Copper Eskimos," *Report of the Canadian Arctic Expedition, 1913–1918*, 12, pt. a (Ottawa: F. A. Acland, 1922), 5–277.

Rasmussen, Knud, *Across Arctic America, Narrative of the Fifth Thule Expedition* (New York: G. P. Putnam's Sons, 1927).

Stefansson, Vihjalmur, *My Life With the Eskimo* (New York: The Macmillan Co., 1913).

Stefansson, Vihjalmur, "The Stefansson-Anderson Arctic Expedition of the American Museum: Preliminary Ethnological Report," APAMNH, 14, pt. 1 (New York: Trustees of the American Museum of Natural History, 1914).

CUNA
Keeler, Clyde E., *Land of the Moon-Children, The Primitive San Blas Culture in Flux* (Athens: University of Georgia Press, 1956).

Stout, David B., *San Blas Cuna Acculturation: An Introduction* (New York: The Viking Fund, 1947).

DOBU
Benedict, Ruth F., *Patterns of Culture* (Boston: Houghton Mifflin Co., 1934).

Fortune, Reo F., *Sorcerers of Dobu, The Social Anthropology of the Dobu Islanders of the Western Pacific* (London: G. Routledge and Sons, Ltd., 1932).

Jenness, Diamond and A. Ballantyne, *The Northern D'Entrecasteaux* (Oxford: The Clarendon Press, 1920).

EGYPTIANS, ANCIENT
Frankfort, Henri, *The Birth of Civilization in the Near East* (Garden City, N. Y.: Doubleday and Co., Inc., 1956).

Kees, Herman A. J., *Das Priestertum im Ägyptischen Staat, vom Neuen Reich Bis zur Spätzeit* (Leiden: E. J. Brill, 1953).

Moret, Alexandre, *The Nile and Egyptian Civilization*, M. R. Dobie, trans. (New York: Alfred A. Knopf, 1927).

Moret, Alexandre and G. Davy, *From Tribe to Empire, Social*

Organizations among Primitives and in the Ancient East, V. Gordon Childe, trans. (New York: Alfred A. Knopf, 1926).

Wilson, John A., *The Culture of Ancient Egypt* (Chicago: The University of Chicago Press, 1951).

GÃ

Field, Margaret J., *Religion and Medicine of the Gã People* (London: Oxford University Press, 1937).

Field, Margaret J., *Social Organization of the Gã People* (London: Crown Agents for the Colonies, 1940).

GANDA

Kagwa, Apolo, "The Customs of the Baganda," Ernest B. Kalibala, trans., May M. Edel (ed.), *Columbia University Contributions to Anthropology*, vol. 22 (New York: Columbia University Press, 1934).

Roscoe, John, *The Baganda, An Account of Their Native Customs and Beliefs* (London: Macmillan and Co., Ltd., 1911).

GENERAL

Murdock, George P., *Our Primitive Contemporaries* (New York: The Macmillan Co., 1934).

HOTTENTOT

Schapera, Isaac, *The Khoisan Peoples of South Africa: Bushmen and Hottentots* (London: G. Routledge and Sons, Ltd., 1930).

IBAN

Freeman, J. D., *Iban Agriculture, A Report on the Shifting Cultivation of Hill Rice by the Iban of Sarawak* (London: Her Majesty's Stationery Office, 1955).

Gomes, Edwin H., *Seventeen Years Among the Sea Dyaks of Borneo, A Record of Intimate Association with the Natives of the Bornean Jungles* (London: Seeley and Co., Ltd., 1911).

Harrisson, Thomas H. (ed.), *Borneo Jungle, An Account of the Oxford Expedition to Sarawak* (London: Lindsay Drummond Ltd., 1938).

Hose, Charles and William McDougall, *The Pagan Tribes of Borneo, A Description of Their Physical, Moral and Intellectual*

Condition with Some Discussion of their Ethnic Relations, 2 vols. (London: Macmillan and Co., Ltd., 1912).

IFALUK
Burrows, Edwin G. and Melford E. Spiro, *An Atoll Culture, Ethnography of Ifaluk in the Central Carolines* (New Haven: Human Relations Area Files, 1953).

IFUGAO
Barton, Roy F., "Ifugao Law," UCPAAE, 15, no. 1 (1919), 1–186.

Barton, Roy F., "Ifugao Economics," UCPAAE, 15, no. 5 (1922), 385–446.

Barton, Roy F., "The Religion of the Ifugaos," MAAA, no. 65 (1946).

IROQUOIS
Hewitt, John N. B., "Iroquoian Cosmology," Smithsonian Institution, Bureau of American Ethnology, vol. 21 (1903), 127–339 and vol. 43 (1928), 449–819.

Morgan, Lewis H., *League of the Ho-de-no Sau-nee or Iroquois*, 2 vols. (New Haven: Human Relations Area Files, 1954).

Stites, Sara H., *Economics of the Iroquois* (Lancaster, Pa.: The New Era Printing Co., 1905).

Wolf, Morris, *Iroquois Religion and Its Relation to Their Morals* (New York: Columbia University Press, 1919).

ISRAELITES
Albright, William F., *From the Stone Age to Christianity, Monotheism and the Historical Process* (Garden City, N. Y.: Doubleday and Co., Inc., 1957).

Johnson, Aubrey R., *Sacral Kingship in Ancient Israel* (Cardiff: University of Wales Press, 1955).

Pedersen, Johannes, *Israel, Its Life and Culture*, 2 vols. (London: Oxford University Press, 1946).

Weber, Max, *Ancient Judaism*, Hans H. Gerth and Don Martindale, trans. (Glencoe, Illinois: The Free Press, 1952).

KAREN
Marshall, Harry I., "The Karen People of Burma: A Study in Anthropology and Ethnology," *The Ohio State University Bulletin*, 26, no. 13 (April 29, 1922).

KASKA

Honigmann, John J., *Culture and Ethos of Kaska Society* (New Haven: Yale University Press, 1949).

Honigmann, John J., *The Kaska Indians, An Ethnographic Reconstruction* (New Haven: Yale University Press, 1954).

LENGUA

Grubb, Wilfred B., *An Unknown People in an Unknown Land* (London: Seeley, Service and Co., Ltd., 1913).

Metraux, Alfred, "Ethnography of the Chaco," HSAI, 1, 197–370.

LEPCHA

Gorer, Geoffrey, *Himalayan Village, An Account of the Lepchas of Sikkim* (London: Michael Joseph Ltd., 1938).

LOZI

Gluckman, Max, "The Lozi of Barotseland in North-Western Rhodesia," STBCA (1941), 1–93.

Gluckman, Max, *Essays on Lozi Land and Royal Property* (Livingstone: Rhodes-Livingstone Institute, 1943).

Turner, V. W., *The Lozi Peoples of North-western Rhodesia* (London: International African Institute, 1952).

MARQUESANS

Linton, Ralph, "Archaeology of the Marquesas Islands," *Bernice P. Bishop Museum Bulletin*, no. 23 (Honolulu: The Museum, 1925).

Linton, Ralph, "Marquesan Culture," in Abram Kardiner, *The Individual and His Society, The Psychodynamics of Primitive Social Organization* (New York: Columbia University Press, 1939), 137–96.

Melville, Herman, *A Narrative of Four Months' Residence among the Natives of a Valley of the Marquesas Islands* (London: J. Murray, 1846).

MIAO

Graham, David C., "The Customs of the Ch'uan Miao," *Journal of the West China Border Research Society*, 9 (1937), 13–70.

Mickey, Margaret P., "The Cowrie Shell Miao of Kweichow," PPMAAE, 32, no. 1 (1947).

NANDI
Huntingford, G. W. B., *The Nandi of Kenya, Tribal Control in a Pastoral Society* (London: Routledge and Kegan Paul Ltd., 1953).

NEZ PERCÉS
Haines, Francis, *Red Eagles of the Northwest, The Story of Chief Joseph and His People* (Portland, Oregon: The Scholastic Press, 1939).

Haines, Francis, *The Nez Percés: Tribesmen of the Columbia Plateau* (Norman: University of Oklahoma Press, 1955).

NUER
Evans-Pritchard, Edward E., *The Nuer, A Description of the Modes of Livelihood and Political Institutions of a Nilotic People* (Oxford: Oxford University Press, 1940).

Evans-Pritchard, Edward E., *Kinship and Marriage among the Nuer* (Oxford: Oxford University Press, 1951).

Evans-Pritchard, Edward E., *Nuer Religion* (Oxford: The Clarendon Press, 1956).

NYAKYUSA
Connor, R. M. B., "Nyakyusa Pagan Religion," *The International Review of Missions*, 43 (April, 1954), 170–72.

Tew, Mary, *Peoples of the Lake Nyasa Region* (London: Oxford University Press, 1950).

Wilson, Godfrey, "An Introduction to Nyakyusa Society," *Bantu Studies*, 10 (September, 1936), 253–91.

Wilson, Godfrey, "The Nyakyusa of South-Western Tanganyika," STBCA, 253–91.

Wilson, Monica, *Good Company, A Study of Nyakyusa Age-Villages* (London: Oxford University Press, 1951).

Wilson, Monica, *Rituals of Kinship Among the Nyakyusa* (London: Oxford University Press, 1957).

OROKAIVA
Williams, Francis E., *Orokaiva Magic* (London: Oxford University Press, 1928).

Williams, Francis E., *Orokaiva Society* (London: Oxford University Press, 1930).

POMO

Gifford, E. W., and Alfred L. Kroeber, "Culture Element Distributions: IV, Pomo," UCPAAE, 37, no. 4 (1937), 117–254.

Kroeber, Alfred L., HIC, 222–71.

Loeb, Edwin M., "Pomo Folkways," UCPAAE, 19, no. 2 (1926), 149–404.

Stewart, Omer C., "Notes on Pomo Ethnogeography," UCPAAE, 40, no. 2 (1943), 29–62.

ROMANS

Bailey, Cyril, *Phases in the Religion of Ancient Rome* (Berkeley: University of California Press, 1932).

Carcopino, Jérôme, *Daily Life in Ancient Rome, The People and the City at the Height of the Empire*, E. O. Lorimer, trans. (New Haven: Yale University Press, 1940).

Coulanges, Fustel de, *The Ancient City* (Garden City, N. Y.: Doubleday and Co., Inc., 1956).

Fowler, W. Warde, *The Religious Experience of the Roman People from the Earliest Times to the Age of Augustus* (London: Macmillan and Co., Ltd., 1911).

Fowler, W. Warde, *Roman Ideas of Deity in the Last Century Before the Christian Era* (London: Macmillan and Co., Ltd., 1914).

Frank, Tenny, *An Economic History of Rome* (Baltimore: The Johns Hopkins Press, 1927).

Homo, Léon, *Primitive Italy and the Beginnings of Roman Imperialism* (New York: Alfred A. Knopf, 1926).

Rostovtzeff, M. I., *The Social and Economic History of the Roman Empire* (Oxford: The Clarendon Press, 1926).

SAMOYED

Czaplicka, Mary A., *Aboriginal Siberia, A Study in Social Anthropology* (Oxford: The Clarendon Press, 1914).

Donner, Kai, *Among the Samoyed in Siberia*, Rinehart Kyler, trans. (New Haven: Human Relations Area Files, 1954).

Jackson, Frederick G., *The Great Frozen Land* (London: Macmillan and Co., Ltd., 1895).

Nansen, Fridtjof, *Through Siberia the Land of the Future*, Arthur G. Chater, trans. (London: William Heinemann, 1914).

Ufer, Heinrich, *Religion und Religiöse Sitte bei den Samojeden* (Erlangen: Verlag von Palm und Enke, 1930).

SHOSHONI

Brackett, Albert G., "The Shoshonis, or Snake Indians, Their Religion, Superstitions, and Manners," *Annual Report of the Board of Regents of the Smithsonian Institution*, 1879 (Washington, D. C.: U. S. Government Printing Office, 1880), 328–33.

Lowie, Robert H., "The Northern Shoshone," APAMNH, 2, pt. 2 (New York: Trustees of the American Museum of Natural History, 1909), 165–201.

Lowie, Robert H., "Sun Dance of the Shoshoni, Ute, and Hidatsa," APAMNH, 16, pt. 5 (New York: The Trustees of the American Museum of Natural History, 1919), 387–410.

Steward, Julian H., *Basin-Plateau Aboriginal Sociopolitical Groups*, Smithsonian Institution, Bureau of American Ethnology, Bulletin 120 (Washington, D. C.: U. S. Government Printing Office, 1938).

Steward, Julian H., "The Great Basin Shoshonean Indians: An Example of a Family Level of Sociocultural Integration," in his *Theory of Cultural Change, the Methodology of Multilinear Evolution* (Urbana: University of Illinois Press, 1955), 101–21.

TALLENSI

Fortes, Meyer, "The Political System of the Tallensi of the Northern Territories of the Gold Coast," APS, 239–71.

Fortes, Meyer, *The Web of Kinship Among the Tallensi, The Second Part of an Analysis of the Social Structure of a Trans-Volta Tribe* (London: Oxford University Press, 1949).

TANALA

Linton, Ralph, "The Tanala, A Hill Tribe of Madagascar," *Publications of the Field Museum of Natural History, Anthropological Series*, 22 (1933).

Linton, Ralph, "The Tanala of Madagascar," in Abram Kardiner, *The Individual and His Society, The Psychodynamics of*

Primitive Social Organization (New York: Columbia University Press, 1939), 251–90.

TIMBIRA
Nimuendaju, Curt, "The Eastern Timbira," Robert H. Lowie, trans., UCPAAE, 41 (1946).

TIV
Bohannan, Laura and Paul, *The Tiv of Central Nigeria* (London: International African Institute, 1953).

TODA
Emeneau, M. B., "Toda Marriage Regulations and Taboos," AA, 39 (January–March, 1937), 103–12.

Emeneau, M. B., "Toda Culture Thirty-five Years After: An Acculturation Study," *Annals of the Bhandarkar Oriental Research Institute*, 19 (January, 1938), 101–21.

Rivers, William H. R., *The Todas* (London: Macmillan and Co., Ltd., 1906).

WINNEBAGO
Radin, Paul, "The Winnebago Tribe," ARBAE, 37 (1923), 35–560.

Radin, Paul and Others, *Der Gottliche Schlem; Ein Indianischer Mythen-Zyklus* (Zurich: Rhein-Verlag, 1954).

YAGUA
Fejos, Paul, *Ethnography of the Yagua* (New York: The Viking Fund, 1943).

YAHGAN
Cooper, John M., "The Yahgan," HSAI, 1, bull. 143, 81–106.

Gusinde, Martin, *Die Feuerland-Indianer*, 2 band, Die Yamana (Mödling bei Wien, 1937).

YOKUTS
Gayton, Anna H., "Yokuts and Western Mono Social Organizations," AA, 47 (July–September, 1945), 409–26.

Gayton, Anna H., "Yokuts and Western Mono Ethnography," *Anthropological Records*, 10, nos. 1 and 2 (1948).

Kroeber, Alfred L., HIC, 474–543.

YUROK

Erikson, Erik H., "Observations on the Yurok: Childhood and World Image," UCPAAE, 35, no. 10 (1943), 257–301.

Kroeber, Alfred L., HIC, 1–97.

Kroeber, Alfred L., "Yurok and Neighboring Kin Systems," UCPAAE, 35, no. 2 (1934), 15–22.

Waterman, Thomas T. and Alfred L. Kroeber, "Yurok Marriages," UCPAAE, 35, no. 1 (1934), 1–14.

ZULU

Gluckman, Max, "The Kingdom of the Zulu of South Africa," APS, 25–55.

Krige, Eileen J., *The Social System of the Zulus* (Pietermaritzburg: Shuter and Shooter, 1950).

ZUNI

Benedict, Ruth, *Patterns of Culture* (Boston: Houghton Mifflin Co., 1934), 57–129.

Bunzel, Ruth L., "Introduction to Zuni Ceremonialism," ARBAE, 1929–1930 (1932), 467–544.

Bunzel, Ruth L., "Zuni Origin Myths," ARBAE, 1929–1930 (1932), 545–609.

Bunzel, Ruth L., "Zuni Katcinas," ARBAE, 1929–1930 (1932), 837–1086.

Eggan, Fred, *Social Organization of the Western Pueblos* (Chicago: The University of Chicago Press, 1950), 176–222.

Kroeber, Alfred L., "Zuni Kin and Clan," APAMNH, 18, pt. 2 (1917).

Parsons, Elsie C., "Notes on Zuni, Part II," MAAA, 4 (October–December, 1917), 229–327.

Smith, Watson and John M. Roberts, "Zuni Law, A Field of Values," PPMAAE, 43, no. 1 (1954).

INDEX